FINDING THE PLOT

a maternal approach to madness in literature

Megan Rogers

DEMETER

Finding the Plot
A Maternal Approach to Madness in Literature
Megan Rogers

Copyright © 2017 Demeter Press

Demeter Press
140 Holland Street West
P. O. Box 13022
Bradford, ON L3Z 2Y5
Tel: (905) 775-9089
Email: info@demeterpress.org
Website: www.demeterpress.org

Demeter Press logo based on the sculpture "Demeter" by Maria-Luise Bodirsky
www.keramik-atelier.bodirsky.de

Printed and Bound in Canada

Front cover artwork and model designs Brigitte May

Library and Archives Canada Cataloguing in Publication
Rogers, Megan, 1979-, author
Finding the plot: a maternal approach to madness in literature / Megan Rogers.
Includes bibliographical references.
ISBN 978-1-77258-136-2 (softcover)
1. Feminist literary criticism. 2. Mentally ill women in literature.
3. Mental illness in literature. 4. Women in literature. 5. Hysteria in literature.
6. Anger in literature. I. Title.

MIX
Paper from
responsible sources
FSC
www.fsc.org   FSC® C004071

For Ava and Maia

Acknowledgements

I owe many debts of gratitude for the support I received during the process of writing this book.

First and foremost I would like to give special thanks to Andrea O'Reilly whose tireless work in maternal scholarship and support of early career academics is a shining light in what can often feel like a darkened room. She is a true and rare maternal mentor.

Dr Craig Batty, for his constant support, guidance, and most of all for his trust that the ideas running around in my head could eventually arrive articulately on the page.

Also and always Dr Antoni Jach who has been my writing (and in some ways life) mentor for more years than I care to mention. Brilliant writer, unequalled bastion of the Australian writing community, Antoni will forever hold a very special place in my heart.

I would also like to thank Maureen Murdock for her time over email and for sharing her thoughts. By writing *The Heroine's Journey*, Murdock became the unwitting herald of my own journey. I am very grateful for her wisdom and words of encouragement.

A very large thank you must be extended to Phyllis Chesler. Phyllis has been an idol of mine for as long as I can remember. I have never met such an intelligent force of nature who is also willing to give her time to others, especially young women. No words would be able to express how grateful I am that Phyllis agreed to read this book and, even more than that, that she agreed to a friendship across oceans. Thank you. Thank you.

Thank you to the amazing artist Brigitte May for designing the book cover and the journey models. Your work is heartfelt, inspirational, and a thing of beauty. Also thank you to my editor Matthew Sidebotham whose keen eye and innate understanding helped me craft my ideas into words.

I would like to thank RMIT University for, so many years ago now, granting me a scholarship and for accepting my doctorate proposal. I am also very appreciative of the support given by the School of Graduate Research, School of Media and Communication, whose financial assistance made possible my visit to Oxford University and The Bronte Parsonage Museum.

My family has, for my whole life, believed in me and supported my education. I would like to thank my father Stuart Brown who raised me to question the mental health system, my sister Andrea Peynenborg for her support and for keeping me grounded, my brother Robert Brown for his support and understanding, my sister Lucette Brown for her love and for always making me laugh, and especially to my mother Sonya Brown for showing me through her own life journey just how strong, resilient, and wonderful a woman can be.

Finally, I would like to thank my husband, Joe, and my daughters, Ava and Maia. My husband is the most amazing and supportive person I could have along for the ride. This book truly would not be here without him. Every day he shows me what an amazing father, husband, and support he is.

And to my daughters, who changed me. Thank you for teaching me what truly matters, for being my muses and for the joy you bring to my life every second of every day. To Ava, for making me a mummy and for teaching me how to truly love, and to Maia for teaching me that love doesn't divide it multiplies. My girls, this is for you.

In a secular age reading fiction is one of the few remaining paths to transcendence, that elusive state in which the distance between the self and the universe shrinks.

—Ceridwen Dovey

Contents

Acknowledgements   5

Introduction: The academic is personal   13

Chapter 1 Who is the madwoman in the attic?   21

The nineteenth-century madwoman   25

Bertha as primary nineteenth-century madwoman   31

The twentieth-century madwoman   33

The twenty-first century madwoman   36

Defining the literary madwomen   38

Literary madwoman as feminist icon   41

Chapter 2 Calls for a new approach   47

Feminist friction   49

Madness and critical disability studies   57

The path forward   61

Chapter 3 Myth and the literary madwoman   69

The monomyth   72

The heroine's journey   74

Separation from the feminine   81

Identification with the masculine   87

Road of trials: meeting ogres and dragons   89

The boon of success   92

Awakening to feelings of spiritual aridity: death   94

Descent to the goddess   96

Madness as narrative closure in the heroine's journey   102

Chapter 4 The eternal madwoman   **103**

A new reading: madness as descent rather than dissent   107

Rupturing the descent/ascent binary   109

Rupture as rebellion   110

Narrative structure as human rather than masculine   121

Chapter 5 Resolving the eternal madwoman   **125**

The eternal madwoman's encounter with darkness   126

Identifying the eternal madwoman's shadow   129

The eternal madwoman and projection   131

The effect of shadow and projection omission   134

The eternal madwoman's attic as liminal space   135

The eternal madwoman as liminal persona   137

Rupture line as borderline   139

Narrative captivity: why the madwoman
remains unresolved   142

Descent and ascent: necessary for narrative   143

Chapter 6 The madwoman's ascent   **147**

The eternal madwoman's individuation and aggregation   148

The key: unlocking maternal agency, unlocking the attic   149

The second crescent: writing the ascent   154

Authority—finding the maternal mentor   155

Autonomy—acknowledging the shadow   158

Authenticity—recognizing and withdrawing projections   160

Empowered maternalism—integrating private and public spheres 161

Chapter 7 The maternal journey   **165**

The modern monomyth   172

Transforming gender ideologies   175

The maternal journey and ordinary language philosophy   177

The maternal journey as postclassical feminist narratology   180

Towards a maternal narratology   184

Chapter 8 Towards an era of reconstruction   187

Reuniting the private and public sphere   192

Reuniting feminist literary criticism with psychoanalysis   193

Reuniting feminist literary criticism with the reader   194

Conclusion   199

Bibliography   205

Praise for *Finding the Plot*   217

List of Figures

Figure 1: Maureen Murdock's model of the heroine's journey   78

Figure 2: The eternal madwoman's journey   105

Figure 3: The heroine's journey and rites of passage   136

Figure 4: The eternal madwoman's narrative captivity   145

Figure 5: The maternal journey   168

Introduction:
The academic is
personal

Many years ago, I attended an academic conference at Oxford University. At the time, having grown up in suburban Australia, the stone buildings and colourful stained glass were intoxicating and the calibre of my fellow attendees gave me a sense of long-sought approval. The three conference days, during which we discussed lofty ideas over white laminate tables by day and debated trends in the humanities over wine in velvety bars by night, were something of a revelation to me. People wanted to hear about my research, asked questions about—challenged, even—its premise and presumptions in intelligent and provocative ways. It was exciting, enjoyable, and deeply reassuring. I had spent the weeks leading up to the conference writing a paper on women's madness in literature— specifically, on the feminist figure of the madwoman in the attic in the form of literary characters such as Antoinette in *Wide Sargasso Sea*, Esther in *The Bell Jar* and the Narrator in *Surfacing*. I argued the madwoman disrupts expected patriarchal plots and serves as a wild alternative to the subservient housewife. Revolutionary, empowering, necessary, she is, I maintained, one of the most important heroic figures in the history of literature.

While writing the paper, I underwent the familiar process of literally climbing up university staircases to discuss my topic with other academics, being inspired and then racing home to research papers, foraging through footnotes and bibliographies, diving deeper and deeper into my topic until the early hours of many mornings. This journey, up in the ivory towers of feminist literary criticism and then down in the *Alice in Wonderland* rabbit holes of research, occurred daily in an obsessive way without much time for anything else. But then, on the last day of the conference, I experienced something that changed my approach to research forever.

I visited a local bookstore to purchase a leather notebook and a special edition of *Surfacing*. Clutching my purchases, I stood behind a well-dressed woman who was talking to a staff member at the counter. In a low voice, the woman asked the cashier if she could please recommend a book or books for her daughter who was trying to navigate a "dark time in her life". The mother explained that her daughter wouldn't read self-help books but that she might read fiction. The staff member had reeled off the usual suspects—*Girl Interrupted, The Bell Jar, Faces in the Water*—when I, being the naively sanctimonious person I could be at that time, spoke up, holding up and suggesting Margaret Atwood's *Surfacing*. The woman looked at me thin-lipped and said something I will never forget: "The woman at the end of that story ends up naked, pregnant, grunting like a pig and completely isolated on an island; do you think that is what I want for my daughter?" The question shocked me. In all the time I had researched the book, and my topic, up in those ivory towers and down those rabbit holes, I had never, not even once, considered the person standing between those two extremities: the reader.

The mother left the bookstore empty-handed, probably partly because of my comment. I often wonder about that woman and her daughter and, in part, this book is for them. But it is also for

my daughters, the daughters being born as you read this introduction and the daughters yet to enter this world. After all, the
personal is political[1] and, indeed, the political is personal and I
believe we have come to a time now in academic writing when it
is impossible to justify any separation of the two interrelated
worlds. In fact, a better catch-cry for research might be that the
academic is personal.

At the time of this experience in the bookstore, my daughter
was two years old and had brought out in me a fierce love,
protective instinct and anxieties about the future. That night I
went back to the room in which my husband, daughter, and
I were staying, just outside Oxford, and I spent all night watching
her sleep. I thought about the characters I considered "madwomen
in attics,"[2] and asked myself: if these characters were (as much of
feminist literary criticism argues) such successful figures of
feminist rebellion, if they should be celebrated and held up on
pedestals as icons, then why was I so reluctant for my daughter
to, as the woman in the bookstore said, have similar experiences?
I kept asking myself throughout that night, surely there is a
better way to rebel in this day and age? Surely a better rebellion
would involve more contentment, more community, and, most
importantly, more empowerment? Surely we had reached a time
in feminist literary criticism when we could climb down from
our ivory towers and crawl up from our rabbit holes to consider
the kind of impact our research has, and could have, on the lived
experiences of real women. These are the questions that fuelled
the writing of this book.

Of course, the traditional definition—indeed, the mainstream
understanding—of academia is that its research does not have
any practical relevance. However, when we look at the
contribution psychology, social science, medical science,
veterinary science, and many of the other Science, Technology,
Engineering and Mathematics (STEM) academic research

programs make, it is difficult not to question the sanctity of such an out-dated definition. There is and always should be a place for purely theoretical thinking, for academics to be free of the confines of economics and the pressures of impact statements. Yet, I do believe that the humanities could more deeply consider its impact and that, to truly survive and thrive, the field will be required to maintain its rigour and increase its relevance. It is also important to remember that once one begins to view literary criticism through a lens such as feminism, one must also consider feminism's own political, social, and humanitarian goals and how they relate to one's research.

After I started considering the impact of my research, I came across an important question raised in Marta Caminero-Santangelo's work in feminist literary criticism, a question that became the focus of this book: "How can the symbolic resolution of the madwoman in fictional texts contribute to the transformation of (rather than just 'resistance' to) gender ideologies?" (181). Caminero-Santangelo argues for feminist practice that improves the lives of real women:

> Instead of privileging the retreat into madness, then, let us privilege forms of agency, and of active transformation in all its forms, which women engage in. And, in doing so, let us open an imaginative space for women to be able to escape from madness by envisioning themselves as agents. (181)

This call has remained largely unanswered. Where are these spaces for characters in feminist literature, which not only represent a way for women to rebel beyond "madness," but also offer an example of the ways this resistance can involve a level of personal and social empowerment? Why do happy endings continue to be not only so unliterary but so damn unfeminist?

As may already be apparent, this book is not written in a traditional academic tone. That is not my authentic style, nor is it,

I believe, the best way to communicate my arguments. In essence, this book is about making academic ideas more relevant and, most importantly, about ensuring research has a positive impact on women's everyday lives. A book expressing this idea in purely academic terms was never going to succeed. In contrast, this book, while drawing on academic thinking and methods, aims to construct and create models that can be used by literary theorists, creative writers of all mediums (novel, screen, play, short story) and maternal theorists to transform the way they read and write female protagonists.

To begin this process, it is important to understand who the madwoman in the attic character is; even though the trope is used in many academic and mainstream publications, there is no clear definition of how we should use and understand the term. Following this definition, I explain how this book will approach and define the terms "madness" and "madwoman" in relation to (and contrast) with the lived experience of real mental illness.

Through the process of understanding the madwoman in the attic, I arrive at a list of the most commonly cited texts including such a character, and focus on the narrative closure or end of these books. By reading the descent of the madwoman through the framework of Maureen Murdock's "heroine's journey" (a revision of Joseph Campbell's hero's journey) we can gain a greater appreciation of the context and psychology that imprisons the madwoman in this figurative attic. Finally, to decipher how— narratively—the madwoman could be released, she is read through the psychoanalytic concepts of individuation and aggregation in the context of maternal agency.

In this way, this book focuses on a specific case at a time when there is what Wittgenstein calls a craving for generality; a requirement to criticize a reading of one, three, or four works as "something inferior, something unsatisfying," as if this is no serious contribution to serious thinking (Moi, 202). Yet, in the spirit of ordinary language philosophy, I do not offer close textual readings as evidence to locate the essence of the literary madwoman in literature, or even in twentieth-century feminist literature; rather, I look more broadly at the madwoman character and the creation of models that could illuminate texts in further studies. What should be welcomed is dialogue with other feminist literary critics to determine whether this specific application could be utilized across historical, class, racial, and national boundaries.

Sadly, dialogue between factions in feminist literary criticism is rare. Over the past forty years, feminist literary criticism has been haunted by hostility. In fact, it is difficult these days to pick up a book, collection of essays, or academic paper that does not summarize the same old animosity between genders, disciplines, approaches, or generations. If Annette Kolodny is not talking about minefields, Elaine Showalter is describing a tumultuous wilderness; if Susan Gubar is not trying to find out who murdered feminist criticism, Nina Baym is predicting the annihilation of sisterhood. And even though these instances occurred in the eighties and nineties, they are still rehashed, reinscribed, or reiterated, leaving the landscape of current feminist literary criticism strewn with bodies and consumed more with fighting one another than with the contribution of new academic theories. My argument with this book is that there is something more important at stake than academic credibility and fragile ego: the day-to-day lived experience of women.

For, in the end, this book is designed to transcend feminism and literary criticism; to be not only a model for an alternate feminist literary criticism, but also a framework for creative writers to construct the next iteration of the madwoman in the attic. Because we should be asking for more than these madwomen dressed up as liberated heroines for our daughters. We should be arguing for a return to literature as storytelling, for novels that give women the ability to experience empowerment vicariously and, in turn, to see with ever-greater clarity the potential of their own lives.

Notes
1   "The personal is political" was a frequently heard feminist rallying cry, especially during the late 1960s and 1970s. The exact origin of the phrase is unknown and sometimes debated. Feminist and writer Carol Hanisch's essay titled "The Personal is Political" appeared in the anthology *Notes From the Second Year: Women's Liberation* in 1970. She is therefore often credited with creating the phrase. However, she wrote in an introduction to the 2006 republication of the essay that she did not come up with the title. She believed "The Personal Is Political" was selected by the editors of the anthology, Shulamith Firestone and Anne Koedt, who were both feminists involved with the group New York Radical Feminists.
2   The notion that some female characters can be considered madwomen in figurative attics is explored in detail in the first chapter. Also explored and defined is the terms "mad" and "madness" and their relationship to "mental illness."

1

Who is the madwoman in the attic?

As a feminist symbol, the raging madwoman is not without controversy. But the power of this image—to cross generic boundaries, inspire resistant readings, and disrupt conventional ideas about sexuality, creativity, myth, history, and narrative—persists not only in the comparatively small house of literary scholarship, but also in many private corners and attics in our so-called feminist world. —Annette R. Frederico (23)

L iterary criticism has always been reluctant to view characters as real people, as if succumbing to the illusion that a character in a book is a person somehow implies losing one's faculties. In 1933, critic L. C. Knights argued that the discerning reader should resist humanist weakness and asked, "How can we maintain the necessary aloofness from a work of art if we treat a character as a human being?" (285). This approach has not only survived, it has become firmly entrenched within the establishment. In literary criticism, distancing a novel from the real world can lead to elitism, but in feminist literary criticism the detachment of female characters from real women can, I would argue, lead to something much more damaging: sacrificing women's empowerment to cerebral metaphor. This is not to say that allegory is not fundamental to literary analysis, but metaphor-based readings put the cart before the horse. Although (as explained later in this chapter) this perspective furthers current critical disability studies, I take the notion of analytical order and couple it with current feminist debate, which questions madness-as-rebellion trope. Feminist literary criticism must view a character as human individual first and metaphor second, so that at the heart of the argument is the understanding that if an environment, situation, or closure would not be seen as politically subversive in the real world, then neither can it be seen to be so in a novel, no matter what that context represents. This approach builds upon a history of feminist literary criticism that aims to "find the woman in the text" (Friedman and Fuchs, 3). Although I believe that a century of literary criticism has found the madness in the text, hardly any have sought to find the woman behind the madness.

Myths about women in society belong to a larger configuration: what Nina Auerbach calls the power of the transcendent, transfigured, and efficacious life of characters in fiction (15). We have identified certain archetypes that transcend character—the damsel in distress, the white knight, the scarlet-letter harlot, the besotted bride—and that have become part of our everyday vernacular. Literary analysis of such characters is a tricky business; often it is difficult to decipher where our personal biases begin and our academic interpretations end. It is a relationship steeped in history and, probably, many assumptions. Often, the theoretical mud we throw at characters sticks and moulds their form and function into something other than that for which they were originally constructed. This is not to say that analysis is a dirty business; on the contrary, literary theory creates paths that flank and cross barriers of the unconscious, that lead to saying what could not be said, that increase our understanding of stories that whisper beneath and between the black letters on a white page. But if we listen, not only to literary characters, but to what literary criticism has told us about them over the years; if we can look at the muddy figure but then peel the layers away to observe anew the naked trope; and, then, if we can examine both in hindsight and with insight, we are able to contribute something altogether new.

One of the most discussed and debated tropes in feminist literary criticism (and, indeed, literary criticism in general) is the character of the "madwoman in the attic"—to the point where, especially in the late 1970s, she achieved almost cult status. Straitjacketed by expectations and, often, by more tangible restraints, the character of the madwoman has been an enormously compelling image of both thwarted feminine potential and society's oppressive assumptions. As a consequence, when the phrase "madwoman in the attic" is used, especially in feminist literary criticism, it is often a disembodied term; the words signify ideas more than an individual. As Nina Baym argues, theorists can be so far convinced by rhetoric as not to see Bertha Mason as a woman. "She" is simply the figuration of anger: "At once true and false; true to the situation of women in patriarchy, but since patriarchy is a false system, witness to its falseness. Her disappearance will simply mark the passing of a false order, not the passing of a female subject" (48).

While depictions and redefinitions of madness are woven through our literature and literary criticism, the madwoman trope is rarely identified as an individual. Therefore, it is important to define, first and foremost, what we mean by the term "madwoman" before we explore the range of her connotations and her position in current feminist literary debate.

I also open with this exploration of the madwoman as

individual, apart from her rebellious connotations, to further work already conducted in current critical disability studies, particularly by Susan Cahn and Elizabeth Donaldson. Critical disability studies argue that the metaphoric interpretation of disability—such as madness—in literature undermines the lived experience of real women encountering emotional distress; that "before we can leap to the metaphor, we need to know the subject. Before we can interpret the semiotics of disability, we need to understand the subjectivity of being disabled" (Davis, xi).

This approach also aligns with the work of Rita Felski, who argues that feminist textual theory cannot simply move from text to world. It must be able to account for the levels of mediation between literary and social domains; in particular, the diverse and often contradictory "ideological and cultural forces which shape processes of literary production and reception" (*Beyond Feminist Aesthetics*, 8). In other words, a feminist literary theory is dependent upon a feminist humanist theory, which must preference fictional characters as social subjects.

Yet, as well as there being a lack of criticism that identifies the madwoman as a subject, there is a lack of texts bringing together the nineteenth, twentieth and twenty-first century examples of literary madwomen. In fact, often when critics mention madwomen they focus on the text, sometimes not even mentioning the characters' names.

While much feminist literary theory recruits poststructuralism into the service of an anti-identitarian politics, I assume, as Susan Fraiman does, the provisional stability and strategic uses of identity categories, such as "woman." As much as I appreciate those opinions that note such terms' exclusivity and normativity, I employ instead ordinary language philosophy, in which, as Wittgenstein argues, a concept can be given a highly specific definition for a particular purpose. At a moment when feminism and identity politics of any kind are regarded warily—too essentialist for many within the academy, too hostile for those outside it—feminist literary criticism's greatest value may lie in a willingness to give madwomen back their humanity.

The nineteenth-century madwoman

In the second half of the twentieth century, a wave of theoretical, fictional, and biographical discourse, in all its multiplicity, explored the madwoman construct in the nineteenth century. This outpouring was part of the first wave of feminist literary criticism, a period Elaine Showalter describes as focusing on rediscovery; rediscovery, mainly, of texts that had been part of university readings lists for decades but which had not been seen through a gendered lens. Although the seminal literary text— the earthquake that triggered the tidal wave—was Sandra Gilbert and Susan Gubar's *The Madwoman in the Attic: The Woman Writer and the Nineteenth-Century Literary Imagination* (1979), Elaine Showalter's *A Literature of Their Own: British Women Novelists from Brontë to Lessing*—published two years earlier, in 1977—set the stage for the feminist literary studies that transformed the field in the 1980s. Launching a major new area for literary investigation, the book uncovered the long, and long-neglected, tradition of women writers in England. A classic of feminist criticism, its impact continues to be felt today. Although Gilbert and Gubar coined the phrase "madwoman in the attic," Showalter identified the "mad wife" as an archetype and explored the numerous literary examples of the trope in stories such as Maria de Vellorno in *Sicilian Romance*, the unnamed protagonist in *The Yellow Wallpaper*, Rebekah in *From Man to Man*, Maggie Tulliver in *The Mill on the Floss*, Anne Catherick in *The Woman in White* and Martha Quest in *The Four-Gated City*. What Showalter concluded from her character analysis, and from applying psychological theories such as those of Phyllis Chesler to novels, was that the women representing the mad wife motif were not "mad" by any modern or medical standard, but simply displayed behaviour that deviated from the expected feminine role. Although published almost forty years ago, *A Literature of their Own* still represents one of the few studies to take a humanistic, rather than a purely metaphorical, approach to the literary madwoman by identifying her as primarily a female individual.

Yet, undeniably, the most commonly cited text in reference to the nineteenth-century madwoman in the attic trope is Gilbert and Gubar's book, which was nominated for the 1979 National Book Critics Circle Award in Literature, and for the 1980 Pulitzer Prize in General Nonfiction. It was reviewed in over thirty publications in English, gained almost unprecedented critical and popular attention, and transformed our approach to women's writing, feminist critique, and the politics of literary canonization. In the preface to their book, the "moguls" of feminist criticism on literary madness, as Showalter calls them, explain that their study began with a course on literature by women that they had taught together at Indiana University in 1974. During that course, as they read the writings of women such as Jane Austen, Charlotte Brontë, Emily Dickinson, Virginia Woolf, and Sylvia Plath, they were surprised by recurring patterns of imprisonment, claustrophobia, and narcissism. The authors used this analysis to identify the angel/monster trope and to define a distinct female literary tradition of that era, which subsequently motivated new readings and appreciation of feminist texts.

Gilbert and Gubar position the nineteenth-century mad-woman in the attic as an important figure of feminist rebellion—a dark double who stands for the heroine's anger and desire, as well as the repressed creative anxiety of the nineteenth-century woman writer. They believe that, trapped within a male-dominated society, the writers struggled with an internal rage against their confinement and with a complexity of anxieties they inherited as a result of their confinement. They dealt with these tensions by creating a metaphor, a double for themselves: the madwoman in the attic. It was through this character that these authors demonstrated their belief that any behaviour outside the parameters of patriarchal culture was considered madness. Gilbert and Gubar were the first to publish a diverse commentary on "mad intertextuality," and they subsequently positioned the madwoman character as an enormously compelling image of feminist disobedience and narrative subversion.

In that period, many writers created a dark version of their heroes and heroines. The motif of the double or doppelganger manifested itself abundantly in gothic literature (*Frankenstein*, 1823; *Wilson Wilson*, 1839) and mystery stories (*Jekyll and Hyde*, 1886; *Despair*, 1836), where repressed fantasies asserted themselves with particular vengeance. The novelist who— consciously or unconsciously—exploited psychological doubles, either juxtaposed or related two characters: one representing the socially acceptable or conventional personality, the other externalizing the free, uninhibited, often criminal self. We see this inner duality externalized in Charlotte Brontë's use of Bertha Mason as Jane's double in *Jane Eyre*.

French philosopher, sociologist and historian Michel Foucault states that people in the nineteenth century considered mad were those who demonstrated (what was believed to be at the time) behaviour "fundamentally alien to the norm" (xviii). For the social institutions and the powers that organized internment (whether in an institution or at home), the mad were guilty because they had made the choice to reject nature. This supposed rejection of what is good and expected, even an acceptance of the devil, are reflected in the mythological names given to characters such as Bertha. There are, indeed, many legends of the madwoman in the attic that express a cultural attitude toward female passion as a potentially dangerous force that must be punished and confined. Showalter identifies a strong mythological aspect to the madwoman in the attic construct; Bertha, for example, is called a vampire, a demon, a witch, and a hag. Each of these is a traditional figure of female deviance with its own history in folklore; both the vampire, who sucked men's blood (as Bertha does when she stabs her brother), and the witch, who visited men by night and rode them to exhaustion, were the products of elemental fears of women.

Three years after Showalter, Nina Auerbach published *Woman and the Demon: The Life of a Victorian Myth,* a study of myths of womanhood, in which she questions the usual generalizations about the squeezed, crushed, and ego-less Victorian woman. Yet Auerbach's examples of literary madwoman are limited; in fact, her text is a good example of a study that perpetuates the trope of the literary madwoman while drawing on examples from other genres and mediums—poets, Anglican sisterhoods and Magdalen homes, bardolatry and the theatre, Pre-Raphaelite paintings, and contemporary cartoons and book illustrations. Reinterpreting a medley of fantasies, she argues that female powers inspired a vivid myth central to the spirit of the age:

> *Once we have reconstructed the Victorian woman and restored her to her demon, I hope we shall find that we have not, after all, stitched together a monster from fragments of bodies, but that we have resurrected a hero who was strong enough to bear the hopes and fears of a century's worship.* (10)

In contrast, while Nancy Armstrong's *Desire and Domestic Fiction* mirrors Auerbach's attribution of the appearance of the demonic woman to a myth that peopled the Victorian world with female demons and angels, Armstrong makes explicit reference to women's madness in literature and focuses on the argument that the novels and non-fiction written by and for women in eighteenth- and nineteenth-century England paved the way for the rise of the modern English middle class. She also concludes that domestic novels of the late 1840s characteristically displayed a madwoman at their centre. Lady Audley in *Lady Audley's Secret*, the protagonist in "The Yellow Wallpaper" and Edna Pontellier in *The Awakening* all embody this demonic persona, and all three heroines embody the fear (which pervaded middle-class culture) that women were "wild beasts" whose lusts and licentiousness ran riot if not constrained by the patriarchal family.

Like *Jane Eyre*, *Lady Audley's Secret* reflects the contemporary medical theory that women were prone to madness due to reproductive instability, an instability that can be inherited by daughters from their mothers. Lady Audley's strange actions date from the birth of her son and the onset of puerperal fever (childbirth was considered a time when women were particularly prone to mental instability). The question of Lady Audley's madness—is she mad or simply wicked?—is one of the key dynamics of the narrative. It is apparently resolved at the end of the book, when she is incarcerated in a private lunatic asylum because she cannot be contained within the bounds of proper femininity. She is the angel in the house turned into domestic horror.

The protagonist in "The Yellow Wallpaper" also transforms from wife and mother into (like Bertha Mason) a captive in her own house. For Gilman, the conventional nineteenth-century middle-class marriage, with its rigid distinction between the domestic functions of the female and the active work of the male, ensured that women remained second-class citizens. The story reveals that this gender division had the effect of keeping women in a childish state of ignorance and preventing their full development.

Similarly, Edna in *The Awakening* is expected to perform her domestic duties and care for the health and happiness of her family at the expense of her own wants and needs. Even though Edna begins to discover her own identity and acknowledge her emotional and sexual desires, this new language is hers alone and, in the end, she is forced to acknowledge the profundity of her solitude. *The Awakening* is a story about Edna's inherent need to speak, and to have her story told; and Edna's tragedy is that she finds that what her story says is unacceptable in her culture and that, in order to live in society, she must silence herself.

After the initial wave of literature and literary analysis in the 1970s, Helen Small published *Love's Madness: Medicine, the Novel, and Female Insanity, 1800–1865*. Concentrating on a specific form of hysteria—love-madness—Small places female mental illness in its historical and theoretical perspective. Within the text, Small studies novels by Jane Austen, Sir Walter Scott, Charlotte Brontë, Wilkie Collins, and Charles Dickens. Through their popular stories of women who go mad when they lose their lovers, Small demonstrates the change in focus from the madman in chains to the crazed woman. Small argues that, after the eighteenth-century cult of sensibility lost literary and social favor in the nineteenth century, the image of the love-mad woman acquired different meanings in novelistic discourse; authors manipulated the convention to express a variety of different social, cultural, domestic, and political stories. For Collins and Dickens, writing at a time when powerful sections of the medical profession were increasingly insisting that knowledge of human life be grounded in physiology rather than psychology, the love-mad woman provided a means of asking what constituted real pain. As Small argues, by understanding how women suffer directly by men's falsehood or, indirectly, by the world's inability to guarantee their happiness, we can get to the truth (220).

Bertha as primary nineteenth-century madwoman

While various characters are identified as embodying the madwoman in the attic motif, Bertha Mason in *Jane Eyre* remains the most commonly cited literary example. Gilbert and Gubar explain that Bertha inspired the name of their seminal text; they felt she, more than any other character, provided them with a "paradigm of many distinctively female anxieties and abilities" (xiii). Bertha is certainly a striking figure of nineteenth-century fiction. Even though she appears in only a few pages of the book—and never actually speaks—literary commentary on the cause of Bertha's madness has been considerable. Brontë described her as a demon, a vampire, and a clothed hyena, but who exactly was Bertha Mason?

What we *are* told is that she is Rochester's clandestine wife, a formerly beautiful and wealthy Creole woman who has apparently become insane, violent, and bestial. It is implied that this "insanity" has been inherited from her mother. She lives locked in a secret room on the third story of Thornfield and is guarded by Grace Poole, whose occasional bouts of inebriation enable Bertha to escape. A character with no dialogue and a peripheral role, she eventually burns down Thornfield, plunging to her death in the flames.

When I started writing this book, I visited the Brontë Parsonage Museum in Haworth to speak with Collections Manager Ann Dinsdale about Bertha. I wanted to discuss and debate the question of whether Brontë created Bertha purely as a character who demonstrated social attitudes towards women and madness at the time. Certainly Brontë created the character Jane Eyre to unsettle views about acceptable women's behavior. It is with Jane that Brontë demonstrates a different, rebellious, and empowering journey. Brontë herself attributes Rochester's first wife's behaviour to "moral madness" (Barker, 383), yet I have often wondered whether she, either knowingly or subconsciously, constructed Bertha as a rebel against social, cultural, and feminine restraint.

At the end of my visit to the museum, I came to a narrow, crowded room to sit with Ann Dinsdale and explore Bertha Mason in more detail. We sifted through stalagmites of papers and glass boxes of books; we took a magnifying glass to the tiny pages on which Brontë would write when paper was scarce; and we wore white gloves to open creased letters she wrote to family and friends. I read author notes on Bertha, perused small books the writer was given at school that describe "exotic natives" and their "mental instability," and spoke to Ann about the fact that Brontë's depiction of Bertha mirrors historical descriptions of mental illness, such as those she would have found in the family's volume of Modern Domestic Medicine.

Through Rochester, Brontë believes Bertha is a victim of a history of maternal madness, the "true daughter of an infamous mother" who was "both a madwoman and a drunkard." In fact, Brontë offers several explanations for Bertha's madness, all taken from the discourse of Victorian psychiatry. Brontë's account echoes the beliefs of Victorian psychiatry about the transmission of madness: since the reproductive system was the source of mental illness in women, women were the prime carriers of madness, twice as likely to transmit it as fathers.

In her own letters, Brontë described Bertha Mason's disease as a "phase of insanity ... in which all that is good or even human seems to disappear from the mind, and a fiend-nature replaces it." What is most notable about Brontë's first representation of female insanity, as Showalter has also argued, is that Jane—unlike the contemporary female critics who have interpreted the novel—never sees her kinship with the confined and monstrous double, and that Brontë has no sympathy for her mad creature. Before Jane can reach her happy ending, the madwoman must be purged from the plot, and passion must be purged from Jane herself.

While many of the Creole character's attributes can be traced back to social depictions of madness at the time, and certainly the belief that anyone culturally different was considered other, there is nothing to imply that Brontë utilized madness as a metaphor for rebellion. What she was doing, rather, was contributing to the ongoing, social dialogue about madness.

English physician James Cowles Prichard defined psychiatric norms during the 1800s when he coined the term "moral madness." Prichard described this illness as a type of madness characterized by "a morbid perversion of the natural feelings, affections, inclinations, temper, habits, moral dispositions, and natural impulses, without any remarkable disorder or defect of the intellect, or knowing and reasoning faculties, and particularly without any insane illusion or hallucination" (Showalter, 29). Such a definition could be stretched to encompass almost any behaviour regarded as abnormal or disruptive by community standards; in general, it meant a perversion of the moral sense and was characterized by what was deemed antisocial behaviour and a lack of self-control.

It was within this environment that Brontë wrote *Jane Eyre* and demonstrated, through Bertha, the dominant social attitude toward cultural otherness and female passion as potentially dangerous forces that must be punished and confined.

The twentieth-century madwoman

Although Bertha Mason is a product of her times, she became the muse—acknowledged or unconscious—of many a twentieth-century writer. As Showalter notes, "to contemporary feminist critics, Bertha Mason has become a paradigmatic figure," and they demonstrate "a sympathy for Bertha that Charlotte Brontë did not seem to share" (124). Many factors, not least the proliferation of feminist criticism and reading practices, have contributed to Bertha Mason's paradigmatic status, and to contemporary readers' newfound sympathy for her.

In 1978, one year after Showalter's *A Literature of their Own* and one year before Gilbert and Gubar's *Madwoman*, Barbara Hill Rigney published *Madness and Sexual Politics in the Feminist Novel: Studies in Brontë, Woolf, Lessing, and Atwood.* Rigney's under-cited book argues against the assumption that psychology and psychiatry impose exclusively male-defined values and standards, and attempts to reconcile feminism and psychology in the area of literary criticism—just as I aim in this work for a similar reunion of psychoanalysis and feminist literary analysis.

Rigney's fertile introduction provides a brief but rich overview of theories about mental illness among women, and her book is one of the few feminist texts to consider the madwoman construct in twentieth-century literature. She reminds us that, from Freud onward, behaviour considered normal and desirable for men is thought to be neurotic, or even psychotic, in women. Through Brontë's *Jane Eyre*, Woolf's *Mrs. Dalloway*, Lessing's *The Four-Gated City*, and Atwood's *Surfacing*, Rigney shows in separate chapters how women's madness in literature is frequently a response to repressive social conditions. Her narrative culminates in a discussion of psychiatrist R. D. Laing's views on madness. Rigney sees Laing's theories as applicable to feminist issues, especially one of his best-known remarks: that psychosis may be the only sane response to an insane society. While Rigney does often focus on the madwoman as metaphor, her argument that the literary madwoman is not mentally ill but is, rather, forced to extremes by her circumstances, mirrors the position of Showalter. While I disagree with some of Rigney's arguments—and particularly her view that madness in literature can be an effective rebellion—I nonetheless aim to further her work in mythic patterns of spiritual journeys and the ways in which these models intersect with psychoanalysis.

Two other texts around this time also considered madness and literature: Marta Caminero-Santangelo's *The Madwoman Can't Speak: Or Why Insanity is Not Subversive* and Shoshana Felman's *Writing and Madness*, which explores the relationship between literature, philosophy, and psychoanalysis through studies of the authors Balzac, Nerval, Flaubert, and Henry James, as well as theorists Michel Foucault, Jacques Lacan, and Jacques Derrida.

Despite the plethora of non-fiction writing about women and madness around this time, for the purposes of this book I have focused on characters in novels written by women. I have excluded memoirs (such as Susanna Kaysen's *Girl, Interrupted*, Kate Millett's *The Loony-Bin Trip*, and Janet Frame's *Faces in the Water*), short stories (such as those by Margaret Gibson), plays (such as Henrik Ibsen's *A Doll's House*), poems (such as those by Emily Dickinson, Anne Sexton, and Sylvia Plath) and published diaries (such as those collected by Jeffrey L. Geller and Maxine Harris in *Women of the Asylum*), although all these have certainly contributed to our perception of the madwoman figure and, indeed, to our understanding of the relationship between women and madness (see Chapter 2).

This focus, or particular case, has been chosen both because there is a significant gap in analysis of the madwoman character as human rather than metaphor in (especially twentieth-century) novels, and because the madwoman motif as rebellious icon is most commonly attributed to characters in feminist literature. For similar reasons, I have chosen wherever possible to list the characters' names and their novels in the text rather than in notes; lists of names may not make for the most compelling reading but I felt it was important to bring these examples to the fore.

Literary characters associated with the madwoman trope in the twentieth century include Lily Bart in *House of Mirth* (1905), Henny Pollit in *The Man Who Loved Children* (1940), Virginia Cunningham in *The Snake Pit* (1946), Istina Mavet in *Faces in the Water* (1961), Esther Greenwood in *The Bell Jar* (1963), Antoinette Cosway in *Wide Sargasso Sea* (1966), Bettina Balser in *Diary of a Mad Housewife* (1967), Marian Mcalpin in *The Edible Woman* (1969), Minn Burge in *The Honeyman Festival* (1970), the Narrator in *Surfacing* (1972), Connie Ramos in *Woman on the Edge of Time* (1976), Cassie Barrett in *The Cracker Factory* (1977), Nora Porteous in *Tirra Lirra by the River* (1978), Agnes Dempster in *Madness of a Seduced Woman* (1984), Sethe in *Beloved* (1987), and Martha Horgan in *A Dangerous Woman* (1991). This list by no means claims to be definitive or exhaustive, but it aims to collate some of the most prominent examples of characters associated with the madwoman archetype in twentieth-century writing.

The twenty-first century madwoman

The madwoman character has survived the nineteenth and twentieth centuries, with many novels published over the last seventeen years containing a similar archetype. These twenty-first century literary madwomen include, but are not limited to: Mathilde Satterwhite in America's 2014 novel of the year, Lauren Groff's *Fates and Furies*, Nora Eldridge in Claire Messud's *The Woman Upstairs*, Amy Elliott Dunne in Gillian Flynn's *Gone Girl*, Jenn in Helen Walsh's *The Lemon Grove*, Yolanda and Verla in Charlotte Wood's *The Natural Way of Things*, Ingrid Magnussen in Janet Finche's *White Oleander*, Arlene in Joshilyn Jackson's *Gods in Alabama*, Simone in Drusilla Campbell's *The Good Sister*, Mrs Sanders in Jayne Pupek's *Tomato Girl*, Gibby McGraw in Lesley Kagen's *Land of a Hundred Wonders*, and Rachel, Anna, and Megan in Paula Hawkins' *The Girl on the Train*.

Mention should also be made of Catherine Lowell's *The Madwoman Upstairs*, which follows protagonist Catherine Whipple as she is sent on a kind of scavenger hunt to solve a literary mystery and untold family legacy, one that can only be unravelled by decoding the clues hidden within the works of the Brontë sisters. There is much intertextuality and reference to the "madwoman" archetype and the character of Bertha Mason; indeed, judged by the title alone, it might be assumed the novel serves as an example of a modern-day literary madwoman. But, in fact, as we follow Catherine along her journey the novel is more an adventure than a *Bildungsroman*; she does not plumb any great depths of sorrow, self-analysis, crisis, or darkness. While the plot is interesting, and Catherine herself a loveable character, the unravelling is of information and plot rather than psychology and character, and although revelations do act as a catalyst for personal reflection by the protagonist, the focus is on external rather than internal development.

While I have excluded short stories from the purview of this work, it is important to note that in this genre, too, the madwoman character captivates writers and readers alike, to such a degree that, in 2014, Rose Yndigoyen edited *Behind the Yellow Wallpaper: New Tales of Madness*, an anthology of short stories inspired by the archetype.

However, despite the persistence of the trope there are three significant differences between the madwomen novels of the twentieth century and those of the twenty-first century. Firstly, and most importantly, the twenty-first century novels are not, for the most part, written specifically in response to the "literary madwoman" character of the nineteenth century; they do not employ madness as narrative rebellion so much as they use madness, or reference to the madwoman, as a genre plot device. This leads us to the second difference: many of these twenty-first century novels are thrillers or mystery novels and, therefore, are focused not so much on the women's journey as on creating suspense and tension. Finally, these novels have not been interpreted by feminist literary criticism as feminist works, or as having subverted power structures with their narrative structure. For the purposes of my analysis, a novel's interpretations are as important as its content; it is not just what the author has included in their writing, but what has been said about that writing, that matters.

One exception to this broad description of twenty-first century works is Claire Messud's Nora Eldridge in *The Woman Upstairs*. Although this book has yet to be interpreted and analysed by feminist literary criticism, it certainly sits within a similar context as the twentieth-century examples and Messud has used a number of intertextual devices to ensure that Nora plays her role in the larger literary madwoman story.

Defining the literary madwomen

From this analysis, we can draw a list of the most commonly cited "madwomen" characters from the nineteenth, twentieth and twenty-first centuries.[1] The nineteenth century encompasses Bertha Mason in *Jane Eyre* (1847), Lady Audley in *Lady Audley's Secret* (1862), the protagonist in "The Yellow Wallpaper" (1892), and Edna Pontellier in *The Awakening* (1899), while the twentieth century saw Esther Greenwood in *The Bell Jar* (1963), Antoinette Cosway in *Wide Sargasso Sea* (1966), and the unnamed protagonist in *Surfacing* (1972).

The twenty-first century literary madwomen are more difficult to identify as that book, so to speak, is yet to be written. We are just beginning to discuss the aforementioned characters, to see their inclusion in academic literary analyses and to witness their impact on readers and society. As mentioned, most twenty-first century literary madwomen inhabit the thriller genre and so fulfill a different purpose, and require a different interpretation, from their predecessors. Nora Eldridge in Claire Messud's *The Woman Upstairs* (2013) is the exception to this rule.

By assembling the feminist madwomen most commonly cited over the last three decades, we can extrapolate certain characteristics both within and across each century and begin to delineate this "particular case" and give definition to the hitherto amorphous nature of the madwoman trope.

In the nineteenth century, what I will now define as the "literary madwoman"—rather than the "madwoman in the attic"—was not always the protagonist of her story, but sometimes a peripheral character, as in the case of Bertha Mason. Therefore,

I define the nineteenth century literary madwoman as, "A female *character*, created by a female author, and interpreted by feminist literary criticism as a rebellious trope whose circumstances cause a breakdown that is about the literal or figurative confinement, or even death, of the self."[2]

In contrast, the literary madwoman of the twentieth and twenty-first centuries is the protagonist of her story, a result of authors wanting to provide women—particularly these previously peripheral characters—with their own narrative. I therefore suggest a definition of the twentieth and twenty-first century literary madwoman as, "A female *protagonist*, created by a female author, and interpreted by feminist literary criticism as a rebellious trope whose circumstances cause a breakdown that is about the literal or figurative confinement, or even death, of the self."

In this way, the term "literary madwoman"—and all phrases in which I henceforth utilize the term "madwoman"—distance themselves from conventional medicalized and gendered notions of mental illness. What I suggest is that the literary madwoman's (specifically) mental instability *is* and *has been* caused by her historical experiences and current circumstances. I therefore stand between two schools of thought about mental illness in academic criticism: on the one side, the disabilities studies approach that argues that madness is a disability represented by real people's lived experience and should not be seen as a metaphor and, on the other, the antipsychiatry movement that insists that mental illness is a myth. While commenting on all examples of mad characters in literature is beyond the scope of this book, what I will argue is that the literary madwoman, including Bertha, is victim of certain experiences—abuse, control, and thwarted desires—that contribute to their mental health. Yet I would also argue, along with Donaldson, that it can be tempting to fall back on concepts of mental illness as a purely social artefact;

that "the true radical challenge that Bertha Rochester represents is far more complex. Ideally, this is a challenge that the next wave of madwoman theory will begin to address" (107).

Although I propose a substantially unchanged definition of the literary madwoman across three centuries, I would argue that the interpretation of the trope by feminist literary critics has evolved dramatically over time. The madwoman character, while remaining a metaphor for feminist disobedience and narrative subversion, has moved from negative to positive; from a mourning to a celebration. Whereas in the interpretation of nineteenth century literary madwoman there is an inevitability to the female character's emotional distress, in the interpretations of the twentieth and twenty-first century literary madwoman there is a level of choice associated with her state of mind. Contemporary feminists revel in the characters' madness in a manner utterly unlike that of their earlier counterparts. Overall, feminist literary criticism of the literary madwoman has changed from what Showalter defined as a rediscovery, to a reorientation; that is, a reorientation of our perception, of the use of and the inevitability of madness. This reorientation not only heralded a change in narrative perspective, it revealed an ambiguity in authorial and reader judgement. The previously silenced and socially undesirable was suddenly favoured, no longer assigned a negative value. It is this reorientation of madness, its celebration as rebellious pathway, and the subsequent worship of the madwoman in the attic trope as feminist icon, which altered radically the structure of feminist literature.

Literary madwoman as feminist icon

Feminist literary criticism seized upon the image of the madwoman as a powerful feminist motif of rebellion and rage and has not let go. But what, we should ask ourselves, underlies the longevity of this character's influence? The attachment has been, in part, a consequence of influential second-wave feminist theory and its continuing stranglehold on current feminist literary criticism. New French Feminism, a movement that emerged after the student revolt of 1968, is particularly interested in how language performs a symbolic function that privileges men, and seeks ways to, as Julie Rodgers phrases it, "subvert the conventions of what they consider to be patriarchal language" (911). Arguing that men, who have historically controlled most of the production of language, have privileged rationality, theorists such as Julia Kristeva, Luce Irigaray, and Hélène Cixous advocate a language of non-reason, with its disruption of oppressive patriarchal thinking and supposed enactment of feminine power.

Cixous defines this approach to writing as *écriture féminine*, loosely translated as "feminine writing." She first used this term in her essay, "The Laugh of the Medusa," in which she asserts, "woman must write her self: must write about women and bring women to writing, from which they have been driven away as violently as from their bodies" (875). Within this feminine writing, Kristeva argues that Western philosophy is founded on the repression of difference. Anything that deviates from the prescribed norm is labeled criminality, perversion, or madness and is prohibited. Thus, in language, female difference is suppressed and the male norm remains as the sole voice. Because the subjective woman does not exist in the male view—she is other, different, lacking—it follows that woman as a speaking "I" does not exist in language. This is why the French feminists argue that, even in language, woman is mute. In turn, French feminism sought to provide previously silenced women with a voice, and, since they felt this was not possible with male language, a new voice emerged; a uniquely feminine style of writing, characterized by what Fiona Tolan describes as disruptions in the text: gaps, silences, puns, and rhythms (328).

Christiane Makward, one of the important translators of and

commentators on French feminism, describes the female lang-uage as open, nonlinear, unfinished, fluid, exploded, fragmented, polysemic, attempting to speak the body (i.e., the unconscious), involving silence, and incorporating the simul-taneity of life, as opposed to—or at least clearly different from—preconceived, oriented, masterly, or didactic languages.

Central to *écriture féminine*, therefore, is the concept of disruption: most prominently the disruption of binaries and narrative structure. Cixous describes the process by which male reason is ordered as a series of binary oppositions in which one half is always superior to the other: male/female, activity/passivity, culture/nature. Irigaray counters this binary structure in her essay "The Sex Which Is Not One" by undermining the masculine binary system of positive/negative and by arguing that the female is not a unified position but multiple positions.[3] *Écriture féminine* also encourages the use of antilinear structure as a way of disrupting the masculine linear, logical, and realistic plot. In this way, patriarchal structure is seen as symbolic, whereas feminine writing is semiotic, threatening to "unleash chaos where there is order" (Tolan, 336). In fact, Cixous argues that hysteria is one of the greatest forces a writer can use to dismantle structure. Therefore, texts that provide primacy to madness (or hysteria) in their narrative could be seen as being sympathetic to the ideals of French feminist criticism.[4] Thus, I will use the term "French feminist criticism" to also mean "New French feminism."

Around 1981, French feminist theory and criticism mobilized madness—dissociated from its clinical categorization—as feminism by promoting the figure of the madwoman as redemptive. They believed and argued that she is not what women have regrettably been reduced to by a contemptuous and oppressive culture; she is, rather—as Cixous argues—what "women either essentially are, or have fortunately been allowed to remain, in a society that brackets but cannot obliterate the innate disruptive, revolutionary force of the female" (48).

For an intellectual wave focused on women's liberation, madness was seen as just one way in which a previously patriarchal mechanism could be embraced as liberating. While the first wave saw madness as almost unavoidable, a necessary evil so to speak, the second wave redefined madness as sitting within the realm of feminist rebellion. Madness was not just represented in literature, as it was during first-wave feminism; it was revered.

As Susan Rubin Suleiman explains in an introduction to Cixous's writing, contemporary feminist theorists no longer refer to new French feminism; no one "does it anymore" (vii).

But, while the term may not be in vogue anymore, the belief that madness in literature, and more specifically the supposed madness of a female character, can actually provide freedom— freedom against a patriarchal society, male language, the constraints of gender stereotypes both in society and writing—is a belief to which Cixous and many feminists and feminist literary critics still cling.

Within this environment, which continues to associate women with madness and feminism with irrationality, feminists are still encouraging the reclamation of hysteria; as a space for marking feminist reaction and resistance to patriarchal oppression, operating as what Cecily Devereux calls a new manifestation of feminism at this moment (21). In her 2014 paper, Devereux argues that the reclamation of hysteria in second-wave feminism was a critical practice whose radical possibility was suspended in the 1990s shift to a foreclosing "post." Now, she argues, hysteria is back; what Mark Micale in 1995 called the new hysteria studies have begun to multiply, and something that we might call the "new" new hysteria studies has emerged in academic study. While Devereux offers an insightful and detailed description of the ways in which the relationship between feminism and hysteria represents important moments in their histories, her ultimate argument is for the future reinvigoration of the term hysteria. She argues:

> What is needed in the new hysteria studies, in this installment of "hystery," is a return to the principles of the late twentieth-century "reclaiming" of hysteria—or, at any rate, to that desire to make radically new definitions and histories and to find a cure for what is still in the end, even (and maybe more emphatically) in the context of renaming, patriarchy's dis-ease enacted in women's bodies. (42)

Devereux's new new hysteria studies has at its core some salient goals: to end debate around women's right to abortion and birth control, punishment of women for going back to work (though she overlooks the right to choose to stay at home), the subjection of women to sexual assault (though she overlooks domestic violence), and the overall call to end the naming of women who do not "play the game" as hysterics. Yet, as Devereux argues for the reclamation of hysteria, feminists around the world are questioning what they believe is the romanticization of a constraining subject. It is this divide, between those second- (and now third-) wave feminists who embrace hysteria and women's madness as a rebellious force, and those second-wave feminists who decry the mobilization of madness that is, I would argue, contributing to a theoretical paralysis in feminist literary criticism.

Notes

1   The texts I have chosen across the nineteenth, twenty and twenty-first centuries are written by women; since the madwoman has so often been defined as a gendered double figure, the writer and character must both be women. This therefore excludes Gustave Flaubert's *Madam Bovary*, Bram Stoker's *Dracula*, and Wilkie Collins's *The Woman in White*.

2   This definition is inspired by Kate Zambreno's, *Heroines* (California: Semiotext(e), 2012), 78.

3   It is important to note here, due to the reference to the maternal later in this book, that in the theoretical discourse of the French feminists Kristeva and Irigaray the maternal occupies a central space. Yet I utilise Marianne Hirsch's argument that these two

women's maternal discourse remains 'firmly embedded in structures of representation which place the mother outside or on the margin' (Hirsch, *The Mother/Daughter Plot: Narrative, Psychoanalysis, Feminism*, 173). For this reason, an analysis of Kristeva or Irigaray's maternal research is not included in this study.

4   It is important to acknowledge that a term such as New French Feminism is far-reaching and includes many theories other than the ones included in this book. The term has been used to attempt to transcend *l'écriture féminine* yet be as specific as one can be within a book's limitations. It is also important to note that I after this specific reference I use "French feminist criticism" to encapsulate this approach and approaches.

2

Calls for a new approach

There is no future for a commonality of
women if we cannot traverse the generations.
—Nina Baym (57)

In August 2012, Shulamith Firestone's body was found in her studio apartment on the fifth floor of a tenement walkup on East Tenth Street, New York. The famous feminist activist and author of *The Dialectic of Sex* had been dead for some days. She was sixty-seven and had battled schizophrenia for decades, surviving on public assistance. Susan Faludi, in April 2013, wrote a long piece in *The New Yorker* about the "Death of a Revolutionary" in which she explored Firestone's life, considerable contribution to feminism, and, ultimately, her untimely demise. In the article, Faludi also describes the horrific abuse Firestone suffered at the hands of the men in her family and, later, the men with whom she had relationships, as well as the fractured relationships she developed with fellow second-wave feminists.

Later that year, Anna Mollow took issue with Faludi's article, arguing that it represented everything that made her angry about the relationship between feminism and madness; when "schizophrenia serves as a metaphor for all that was (supposedly) wrong with the second-wave women's liberation movement." In her response, Mollow argues that Faludi suggests that, "if second-wave feminists had only been nicer to each other, Firestone might not have gotten ill." Claiming that schizophrenia is caused by "social isolation," Faludi blames feminists' infighting for perpetuating women's "alienation from each other." Mollow also quotes Merri Lisa Johnson, and explains that they are both frustrated by the "ablenormativity" of many feminist accounts of mental illness and both long for a feminism that "will take mental illness seriously."

While I think Faludi's description of Firestone's mental illness is more nuanced and sympathetic than Mollow will have us believe, these articles and their dialogue represent an historic and ever growing divide in the feminist world, a divide caused by different answers to the questions, how should we, as feminists, talk about madness? And, how should we represent the relationship between feminism and madness? More specifically, one of the longest running divides in feminist criticism focuses on whether madness should be celebrated as effective rebellion. This topic separates, on the one hand, a populist position that seeks to link texts to everyday life practices in the hope of effecting direct social change and, on the other, the preference of an academic feminism that Felski describes as having "a professional commitment to more rigourous and intellectually sophisticated and in turn esoteric forms of analysis" (*Beyond Feminist Aesthetics*, 11).

Feminist friction

One of the primary clashes pertinent to this book is that between those espousing an expressive, and typically content-based, approach that valorizes female consciousness and those, more linguistically focused, who argue that disruption occurs through the very structures of symbolic discourse. In much literary criticism, this dichotomy is referred to as American versus French approaches and I will, for the sake of brevity and alignment with current and historic dialogue, also refer to the two sides in this manner. Yet it is important to note that there are American feminist critics on the French side and vice versa, so that the terms "French" and "American" feminist theory, and the ways in which they are used throughout this book, must be taken to refer to a grounding in a particular intellectual tradition, rather than simply to the nationality of the individual critic. It is also important to acknowledge that adopting this binary nomenclature risks portraying the rival approaches as emanating from two intellectually homogeneous groups, rather than from schools of thought encompassing a range of rich individual variations—although, I would argue, given the clear animosity between them, there is a sense in which the whole of each side is greater than the sum of its parts, however varied. It should also be noted that my approach to the terminology differs from that of those concerned with the standard argument against essentialism.

This dichotomy has created tensions between literary theory and literary practice, between what Felski describes as an "intellectual commitment to questioning fixed positions on the one hand ... [and] forms of writing which often appear to embrace a belief in an essential truth of female experience on the other" (*Beyond Feminist Aesthetics*, 18). In a sense, this tension can be seen as an inevitable consequence of the institutionalization of feminism as an academic discipline. Yet feminism constitutes not only an increasingly sophisticated body of theory but also, as feminist literary criticism often forgets, a political ideology linked to a social movement concerned with processes of change and emancipation.

Recent years have also seen a proliferation of critiques of first-world, heterosexual, middle-class, white, feminism (of which I admit to being a card-holding member). The approaches used throughout this book, such as structuralism and myth criticism, are often applied by the suspension of differences other than those upon which they focus, in this instance gender. Frameworks and arguments made within this book do not necessarily reflect adequately the lived experiences of women as a collective group, nor do they properly take into account race and class biases. Unfortunately, however, in twenty-first feminist literary criticism, one is often damned if one does and damned if one doesn't. If we make what Gubar terms "obeisance to the necessity of considering (without subordinating) race, class, gender, sexuality, and nation," ("What Ails Feminist Criticism," 891) we are criticized for being patronizing, speaking for persons historically lacking a voice and working hand-in-hand with colonialism and imperialism; yet, if we stay in our lane and, as Gayatri Spivak would say, discuss only literary writers who are aligned with what we see in the mirror, we are criticized for generalizations about women's experience, perpetuating the negation of other types of womanhood and, indeed, for working hand-in-hand with colonialism and imperialism. This has led, as Gubar argues, to a fear of saying the wrong thing and, in the end, deathly silence ("What Ails Feminist Criticism," 891).

Although I align myself with the "American" side of the feminist dichotomy, I also argue this approach must evolve and also respect, appreciate, and acknowledge the other side. Though Gubar's diatribe may come across as angry and wounded, there are components of her argument that are possibly, I would argue, even more relevant today. Also pertinent are Phyllis Chesler's words:

> *Relatively privileged white middle-class women discovered that*
> *privilege was not freedom; that love was a foreign country with few*
> *survivors; and that the female body was as colonized as any ghetto*
> *or Third World country. They also discovered that neither men nor*
> *women liked women, especially strong happy women.* (295)

Originally the "we" in women represented a group subordinated to the concept of masculinity; the group viewed by the man as his opposite, his other. In the early decades of feminism, this uniting definition was activated to demand the right to vote, dress reform, birth control, own property, get divorced, and obtain an education. Yet now there is not only hesitation but also condemnation of any reductionist reference to a "we"; the opposites now are not men and women but, within feminist literary criticism, women and women.

When one looks at second-wave feminism's seven main demands (equal pay; equal education and opportunity; contraception and abortion on demand; free childcare; financial and legal independence; freedom from intimidation by threat or use of violence or sexual coercion, regardless of marital status; and an end to all laws, assumptions and institutions that perpetuate male dominance and men's aggression towards women) there is much left to accomplish. Yet feminist criticism, as a whole, has become so consumed by circular logic, intensely theoretical rhetoric and insular, semantic debate in which common goals are criticized, that it has become ineffectual as an oppositional discourse. Rather than building on each other's frameworks, we become trapped in a revolving door of competition: who has been more oppressed? Who has the right to speak about whose experience? And, indeed, whose argument is more authentic? More advanced? More important, even? Instead of bolstering the academic work of another by filling in the theoretical holes they could not possibly address in a single paper, or even a single book, we dismiss any work that is not written to very specific criteria. The result is that we silence other women's voices in a manner, I would argue, very reminiscent of that of the patriarchal culture early feminists fought against. We also end up eliding the diversity of women within western, white, middle-class society.

A prime example of such criticism is that of Gilbert and Gubar's seminal *The Madwoman in the Attic: The Woman Writer and the Nineteenth-Century Literary Imagination*. While the text received widespread support and praise when published, it has not been without its critics. As William Cain explains, "they [Gilbert and Gubar] paid a price for their accomplishments, and have been roughly indicted in tones of voice that are seldom employed for male scholars of comparable importance" (xix). Many scholars willing to open the canon to women authors still resist the feminist insistence that a writer's gender is crucial to her work: "The notion of women who write, read, or teach as women strikes antifeminists as special interest criticism, as cheerleading and propaganda," Cain writes (xix). Yet, for Gilbert and Gubar, later generations of feminists have been among their sternest critics. They accuse the professors of speaking too broadly, and of ignoring distinctions among women of different races, classes and nationalities. Gilbert and Gubar acknowledged the criticism: "We were cast as establishment puppets just too dumb to notice that we wrote from a position of middle-class, white, heterosexual privilege" (xxv).

Among the most famous retorts was that of Gayatri Chakravorty Spivak, who argued that, in ignoring the fact that Bertha Mason was a Creole Jamaican, the authors left out of their account the ways in which British imperialism and racism afforded privileges to white women. In Spivak's rendering, Bertha's attic stands in for the marginalized third world; thus, the whole book is really about nineteenth-century middle-class white women. Erin O'Connor has critiqued that essay, arguing that Spivak neither argued nor proved her point but simply declared it—how ironic, O'Connor notes, that in attacking Gilbert and Gubar for propping up imperialism Spivak "rules" (221). Whatever the criticisms of Gilbert and Gubar's text, there is no denying that it is a foundational work, not only for feminism but for literary theory more broadly. I agree with Carol Margaret Davison when she writes:

> The tendency in recent years of third-wave feminists and poststructuralist/deconstructionist critics has been to scoff at and undervalue such scholarship, to demean it as close-minded, archaic, myopic, and essentialist in that it universalizes female identity and experience. While such an inclination has resulted in some provocative scholarship and the development of some useful theoretical paradigms, it is also arrogant and itself myopic. Indeed, this response is akin to laughing at the inventor of writing implements whose experiments gave us the tools with which we write. Although their tools might require reconsideration and refinement, we would be inarticulate without them. (212)

My point here is not that we should return to a past age or ignore areas where arguments could be developed, but rather to propose an alternative feminist literary criticism, one that is able to accommodate focused studies and to build upon, fill in, and balance important studies in literature. In this way, I argue for a more dialectical position that acknowledges both the interrelations and the tensions between literature and feminist politics.

Overall, there is increasing criticism of subversive literary madness and, in turn, a corresponding interest in a literature that has a more empowering and positive message for women. There is a growing belief by academics such as Felski that literature is not merely a self-referential system, but a medium that can "profoundly influence individual and cultural self-understanding in the sphere of everyday life," charting "the changing preoccupations of social groups through symbolic fictions by means of which they make sense of experience" (*Beyond Feminist Aesthetics*, 7).

Felski provides a measured and balanced approach to her analysis and includes a critique of the limitations of Anglo-American feminist criticism, insofar as it tends to rely upon a reflectionist theory of literary meaning and is unable to theorize adequately the significance of modernist and avant-garde texts in the context of the development of literary form. Although I agree with Felski's criticism, I also argue that French feminist criticism, which believes that complex structures of literary form and language undermine, distance, or otherwise call into question the fixed meanings of ideology, has its own limitations. These blind spots, based on assumptions of the masculinity of narratology and psychology, are outlined later in this book. Although I align myself with American feminist criticism and the arguments by theorists in this chapter, I also aim to acknowledge and embrace components of the French feminist approach and, in this way, to mitigate the disciplinary fissures between an empirical sociology or history on the one hand and a purely textualist literary theory on the other. Rather than aiming at the construction of a single, comprehensive feminist literary theory, I focus on the resolution of the madwoman in literature as a microcosm or particular case of possible emancipation and unification of feminist polarities.

For this understanding to occur, critics of the belief that madness undermines the authority of a "masculine" symbolic discourse must be collated and their arguments explored—which is yet to be done in feminist literary criticism. Over the past almost-forty years, feminists have been calling upon writers, critics, and feminists to respond to the necessity for new narratives about madness but, as yet, no one has responded.

Many feminist critics[1] have argued, and continue to argue, that embracing chaos, madness, and the non-rational as a resistance strategy does little to dismantle the dichotomous thinking decried by French feminist criticism; rather, as Caminero-Santangelo argues, "it simply reverses the poles ... [while] duplicating the essentialist thinking that identifies women with irrationality in the first place" (*The Madwoman Can't Speak*, 3).

There has been a commonly held belief (expressed, for example, by Helen Small in *Love's Madness*) that the division in beliefs about madness is also a division between French feminists and American feminists. This belief was encouraged by Felman's 1975 article in "Women and Madness: The Critical Phallacy," which, at the very outset of the debate, pitted Chesler's belief that madness equals paralysis against Irigaray's belief that madness equals power. It is undeniable that these two academics, and arguments, are poles apart; yet what is often missed is that, even within second-wave French feminism, the glorification of madness has been controversial.

In her debate with Cixous in *The Newly Born Woman*, Catherine Clément was more skeptical about the power of hysteria as a form of feminist subversion. She maintained that "the hysteric is unable to communicate because she is outside of reality and culture" and that hysterics should not, therefore, be classed with feminist heroines but with "deviants and marginals who actually reinforce the social structure by their preordained place on the margin" (66). "You love Dora," Clément said to Cixious, "but for me she never seemed a revolutionary character" (67). In fact, she argues that "in order to affect the symbolic order, or the material world the hysteric must somehow break through her private language and act" (67). Domna C. Stanton, another figure of French feminist theory, argues that recurring identification of the female in *écriture féminine* with madness, antireason, primitive darkness, and mystery, represents a revalorization of traditional feminine stereotypes.

As the above makes clear, the opposing schools in the debate on madness are not clearly delineated; however, over the past twenty-five years American feminist critics have certainly been the most sustained voice against the notion that madness is rebellion. Returning to Felman's article, she writes that:

> depressed and terrified women are not about to seize the means of production and reproduction: quite the opposite of rebellion, madness is the impasse confronting those whom cultural conditioning has deprived of the very means of protest or self-affirmation. Far from being a form of contestation, mental illness is a request for help, a manifestation both of cultural impotence and of political castration. (20)

Baym mirrors this criticism, questioning the use of the madwoman-as-rebellion motif by feminist critics and underlining how their treatments have served to uphold the "hegemonic mindset that recapitulates and hence capitulates to fear, dislike, and contempt of women" (282). Baym takes a practical approach in her arguments, explaining that it is all well and good for academics in their ivory towers to expound the use of the nonlinear, exploded, fragmented, polysemic speech associated with the madwoman, but that women entering public life, "whether as Supreme Court justices or organizers of tenants' unions, disprove the theory empirically, and indeed would follow it at their peril" (49). Baym argues that any support of madness as effective rebellion does not merely affirm belles-lettres as an elite pastime; it relegates women to uselessness.

Makward also stresses the powerlessness of the madwoman motif when she writes that the theory is dangerously close to repeating in deconstructive language the traditional assumptions: "It is an essentialist definition making women incapable of speaking as a woman; women are resigning themselves to silence, and to nonspeech. The speech of the other will then swallow them up, will speak for them" (100).

Although the association between rebellion and madness has enabled feminist critiques of the gendered politics of psychiatric diagnosis, another interpretation argues that the mad subject holds little political power. This is not to say that accounts of female madness, which provide a voice to the gendered experience, have not been significant for society, feminism, and literary studies. But exposing the reality of women's experience is not the same as interpreting those stories as representing the liberating potential of language.

While American feminist criticism has hitherto offered the most sustained resistance to the madness-as-rebellion trope, in recent years an influx of critical disability studies theorists have become the loudest voice denouncing the notion of irrationality as subversive and questioning the ways in which this approach entirely unmoors the literary madwoman from any associations with mental illness.

Madness and critical disability studies

The diversification of critical social theory in recent years has opened up new modes of critical enquiry. Despite this, there are certain principles that align disability studies arguments with the arguments made about the literary madwoman by feminist literary critics. Disability studies present a number of arguments very different to any made by psychologists, literary critics, or feminists. As emancipation is a cornerstone of critical theory, I often utilize a critical disabilities studies (CDS) approach.

Lennard J. Davis's *The Madwoman and the Blindman*, published in 2012, was the first work to approach the literary madwoman—in this case examining just one example, *Jane Eyre*—from a disability studies perspective. This text represents a defining moment in the literary madwoman's evolution, when she, her madness, and any connotation of rebellion this madness possesses is engaged with by a group of scholars in a new field of study. In fact, Davis described the text as a "coming of age moment in disability studies" (ix).

Yet, although offering a new and interesting perspective, this work and its authors were nonetheless writing at a time when the scholarship (postcolonial, feminist, literary, Marxist, psycho-analytical) on *Jane Eyre* was well established, diverse, and dense. As I well know, it is difficult to make advances in the interpretation of the novel and its madwoman in the attic character, and Davis's compilation of essays fails perhaps as often as it succeeds. Probably the most successful new interpretation is that of Julia Rodas, who reads the novel through the lens of autism. In a thoughtful and fruitful analysis, she not only convinces us to look not only at Jane in new ways—as demonstrating many autistic traits—but also other characters in the novel.

Also interesting is Davis's exploration in the opening chapter of metaphor, in which he argues that the process of metamorphosis is a substitutive one in which one says that something is something else—for example, that a woman is a rose, or that a scythe is death—and that this process is designed to distract and to disengage the reader. For, when we say a woman is a rose, we are "looking away from the woman and toward the rose and saying that roses smell sweet, look beautiful, and are fecund" (x). Even more important, and pertinent to this work, is Davis's argument that identity-based readings should succeed—not precede—disabilities studies readings, since (as mentioned in Chapter 1) we should see the madwoman as a woman first, as a real person, before we analyze her in a metaphorical or metacritical reading. Where I align my arguments with those of current disability studies is precisely in this perspective, that the madwoman should be seen as a human being first—and, also, that attitudes toward the madwoman in the attic, like attitudes about 'disabled' people, are historically, culturally, and situationally determined.

What I was more interested in, though, was not new readings of disability in general, or of Jane or Mr Rochester, but specifically new approaches to Bertha Mason and her madness. Initially, I was interested in D. Christopher Gabbard's approach to Bertha and her caregivers, and his application of Nary Louise Pratt's "contact zone" theory to Thornfield's attic. Unfortunately Gabbard's foray into dialogism and interlocutor reads more like historic linguistic scholarship than a forward thinking approach. His study also focuses more on Jane and Rochester and does, at times, seem to be guilty of what Davis describes in the opening chapter of "looking away" from the person with a disability.

The only article to adequately tackle madness as metaphor from a disabilities studies perspective is Donaldson's "The Corpus of the Madwoman." Yet while Donaldson's article is an excellent study, and certainly put disabilities studies on the map from a literary perspective, it is hardly new, having first appeared in the journal *Feminist Formations* in 2002.

In what has become a seminal article in the intersection of literary and disabilities studies, Donaldson argues that the madness/rebellion configuration subtly reinforces what has become an "almost monolithic way of reading mental illness within feminist literary criticism" and perhaps the "larger culture of women's studies scholarship" (101). Donaldson believes that madness as metaphor has problematic implications. Even though Gilbert and Gubar "warn readers against romanticizing madness," Donaldson acknowledges that the figure of Bertha Mason as a rebellious woman subverting the patriarchal order by "burning down her husband's estate has a certain irresistible appeal" (99). But, she argues, madness, however romanticized, offers women little possibility for true resistance or productive rebellion.

Donaldson's arguments do suffer from being part of a new theoretical offshoot, as well as from coming from the social model of disability, which argues for a conceptual distinction between "impairment" as a functional limitation and "disability" as a socially generated system of discrimination. This binary way of thinking about disability, as Helen Meekosha and Russell Shuttleworth argue, has been the subject of critiques by a number of feminists, cultural studies scholars and postmodernists, leading to tensions and splits within the disability studies community, particularly in Britain.[2] Critical disabilities studies is a move away from the preoccupation with binary understandings and would provide a more nuanced and original contribution to thinking about madness as disability in literature.

There are many strengths to Donaldson's arguments, and her work certainly paved the way for some of the ideas behind this book—in particular, that antipsychiatry and conceptions of madness as feminist rebellion are essentially conservative: they do not require a radical rethinking of our central political principles. Tempting though it may be to fall back on concepts that imagine mental illness as purely socially produced, the true radical challenge that Bertha Rochester represents is far more complex. Ideally, this is a challenge that a new wave of madwoman theory, one based on the insights of both feminism and disability studies theory, will begin to address. Thus, I position myself and this book as the next wave of madwoman theory.

Another work by a disabilities studies academic, Cahn's "Border Disorders," is, I would argue, one of the most important, recent articles written about mental illness from a feminist perspective, and one that also argues madness offers little personal or political rebellion. Cahn argues that borderline personality disorder (BPD) has become the twenty-first century hysteria. Building on insights from disability studies about the social construction of illness, and on feminist critiques of BPD, Cahn explores questions of mental illness, the self, and suffering: how do we understand the interplay between corporeal body and the social environment in producing mental suffering? How do we, collectively, work to prevent, ameliorate, or heal severe emotional pain, especially when it is disabling and persistent over time? And, how do we turn harmful gender bias into salutary gender insights? Interestingly, in many ways Cahn's questions mirror those of Caminero-Santangelo. Yet although there are many arguments currently circulating against madness as metaphor, there is little discussion about how effective rebellion might actually look.

The path forward

One reason the madness debate has been so enduring is that no one has, as yet, proposed an effective resolution; the arguments over semantics and effectiveness go around and around but never forward. However, a number of feminist critics are pointing towards new narratives as a way to move the debate forward. Showalter herself, in her later writings, explains that it seems paradoxical that Dora, a notoriously unsuccessful hysteric, should have emerged as a feminist heroine in the 1970s. It is bizarre, she argues, to find Dora put forward as a feminist ideal and saluted by successful writers such as Cixous, given that Dora (although her dream was to become a writer) never found her own voice, and that her supposed rebellion ultimately turned back on itself. Therefore, Showalter argues, Dora's feminist power paradoxically is as a *tragic* literary figure—as is, I argue, the literary madwoman. Feminist critics have taken up the concept of the "hysterical narrative" to describe a story that is fragmented and incoherent. As Toril Moi has pointed out, what Freud describes as the incoherence of the hysteric's story has less to do with the nature of hysteria or the nature of women than with the social powerlessness of women's narratives. The *reason* the neurotic fails to produce coherence is that she lacks the *power* to impose her own connections on her reader/listener.

Caminero-Santangelo mirrors this question in *The Madwoman*

Can't Speak, arguing that Bertha Mason's madness "offers [only] the illusion of power" (3). In her thorough and thoughtful study, Caminero-Santangelo takes aim at the argument that madness is an appropriate and accurate metaphor for socially constructed femininity or for female resistance to dominant ideological constructions. By using both fictional madwomen and women's biographical accounts of asylum experiences, she reveals the limited efficacy of the mad subject and, by providing rereadings and readings of underutilized books, she contrasts asylum narratives by Sylvia Plath and Kate Millet, among others; the figure of the manless madwoman in works by Eudora Welty, Jean Stafford, and Hortense Calisher; multiple personality and the postmodern subject in Shirley Jackson's *The Bird's Nest* and *The Three Faces of Eve*; madness in novels by Toni Morrison; and murdering mothers in works by Morrison, Helena Maria Viramontes, and Cristina Garcia.

Like feminist scholars such as Gilbert and Gubar before her, Caminero-Santangelo demonstrates that there are shared themes, belief systems, and metaphors evident in women's writing about madness and that they all share the premise that insanity is the final surrender to dominant discourses precisely because it is characterized by the (dis)ability to produce meaning. As mentioned previously, Caminero-Santangelo argues that disputing the effectiveness of the figure of the madwoman has created what she calls *the* central question of feminist debate: how can the symbolic resolution of the madwoman in fictional texts contribute to the transformation of (rather than just resistance to) gender ideologies?

Importantly for this book, she also argues for feminist practice that improves the lives of real women:

> *Instead of privileging the retreat into madness, then, let us privilege forms of agency, and of active transformation in all its forms, which women engage in. And, in doing so, let us open an*

> *imaginative space for women to be able to escape from madness*
> *by envisioning themselves as agents.* (181)

Although she demonstrates that the subversive powers of madness can only be theoretical, Caminero-Santangelo turns primarily to *Beloved* to argue that the remembering of stories and the extension of family structures into the larger community, not madness, are the means through which oppressive discourses may best be resisted.

Although it is a successful extended exploration of the variety of ways that madness, gender, race, and social power interact in a range of contemporary women's texts, *The Madwoman Can't Speak* leaves questions unanswered. By tracing the symbolic rejection of disempowering solutions in fictional and non-fictional narratives, Caminero-Santangelo goes some way in responding to her question, but the female protagonists she analyses remain entangled, broken, unclear, and unsettled, the precise opposite of being adequately resolved. Thus, at the end of *The Madwoman Can't Speak*, the dilemma remains of how one writes such a transformational text. Furthermore, while Caminero-Santangelo points to the intersection of studying texts and writing texts, to the combination of theory and practice as a possible answer, we are left unsure as to how this would transpire practically. Her research, therefore, remains as unresolved as the literary madwomen itself. Yet, as explained in the introduction, my aim in this book is to identify gaps in previous feminist literary criticism and, rather than dismiss the theories because of this missing information, celebrate the work as providing important frameworks to build upon and opportunities for further discussion. As such, Caminero-Santangelo's unanswered call for the transformation of madwomen in fictional texts poses an important challenge for this book and provides an opportunity to contribute new knowledge and approaches to feminist literary criticism.

Diane Price Herndl takes Showalter's and Caminero-

Santangelo's questions a step further, arguing that the only way a woman can become the subject of her own story, and thereby transform gender ideologies, is through writing narrative (74). In a play on Freud's "talking cure," Herndl uses Gilman's writing of *The Yellow Wallpaper* and subsequent books, and the way in which it "cured her" (i.e., Gilman), to argue for writing as remedy. Certainly if, as Herndl argues, hysteria is a woman's response to a system in which she is expected to remain silent, a system in which her subjectivity is continually denied, then in becoming a writer a woman becomes not just a subject but a subject who "produces that which is visible" (53). Also, in making her subjectivity seen, writing affords the woman the status of speaking-subject or, as Herndl terms it, language-using-subject. Even more interesting is Herndl's argument that a woman-as-writing subject is also a revision of metaphors; that is, in a male-defined signifying system, the woman who has historically been the subject of literature or the inspiration for literature cannot be the subject who writes; thus, in becoming a writer the woman comes to inhabit a different cultural position a position, which opens new possibilities to her. Ultimately, Herndl argues, to resolve the literary madwoman she must become the writer of her own story, and this re-envisioniong of metaphors opens new possibilities for women at the turn of the century. Although Herndl wrote this advice almost thirty years ago, there has been no real response to—or what I call "activation" of—this argument or research and, therefore, her belief is even more pertinent now than it was in 1988.

Chesler, in the 1975 edition of *Women and Madness*, raised similar questions to Caminero-Santangelo when she asked, how can women banish self-sacrifice, guilt, naiveté, helplessness, madness, and sorrow from the female condition? How can a woman survive—and learn to value survival? Yet thirty years later, in her 2005 revision of *Women and Madness*, rather than

Herndl's "writing cure" Chesler provides (in a more concrete answer than Caminero-Santangelo's encouragement to remember stories) what she feels is a plausible solution: the answer is found in myth, she argues, in the transformational and empowering stories of goddesses, Earth mothers, and Amazon figures. Such narratives are our "collective human role models," she argues, and we "repress them at our own peril" (3). Thus, Chesler's argument is one of not only writing but also one of reading and sharing, a more communal response to resolving the madwoman.

In fact, over the past fifty years there has been a multitude of feminist literature advocating myth as a possible guide for women's self-actualization. Marija Gimbutas's *Language of the Goddess* (1989), Lee R. Edwards's *Psyche as Hero* (1984), Carol Pearson's *The Hero Within* (1986), Maureen Murdock's *The Heroine's Journey* (1990), Kim Hudson's *The Virgin's Promise* (2009), and Valerie Estelle Frankel's *From Girl to Goddess* (2010) all explore myth as a possible framework for a woman's quest for internal growth and change. Gayle Greene's identification of "quest fiction" has also led me to the literary interpretation of myth criticism as a possible way to later examine the narrative structure of twentieth-century feminist literature. Auerbach, Felski, Edwards, and Dana A. Heller have been calling for a return to a focus on myth and, more specifically, a return to a focus on Psyche as hero. They argue that new approaches to the monomyth would fulfil a female protagonist's need for an empowering self-image, and grant her the mobility she requires to imagine, enact, and represent her quest for authentic self-knowledge (Heller, *The Feminization of the Quest-Romance*, 14). Auerbach began moving in this direction in her earlier book, *Communities of Women: An Idea in Fiction* (1978), which uses female communities in Greek mythology to examine novelistic depictions of matriarchal power in groups such as families and schools, and in her previous exploration, *Woman and the Demon: The Life of a*

Victorian Myth (1984). Yet, no academic work has linked the possible resolution of the madwoman in fiction with myth; no work has read, or recommended a reading of, the literary madwoman character using the monomyth framework to determine how she navigates the journey, and to determine whether this analysis provides an answer to her emancipation.

One of the main reasons there has been little response to so many feminists calling for a focus on myth has been the dominance of the French feminist approach in current studies. In fact, the prominent strand of feminist literary criticism over the past forty years, which has had a romance with deconstructionist scepticism, has heavily criticized myth. I argue that the call for subjectivity, spirituality, and myth that emerges from American feminist critics as a significant component missing from feminist literature cannot be unconditionally dismissed as naïve or regressive but, rather, as Felski argues, "calls attention to needs which have been suppressed by prevailing ideologies of modernity and progress and which socialist politics has typically failed to address" (*Beyond Feminist Aesthetics*, 149).

Although I position myself on Chesler's side of the feminist divide, arguing that madness can never be a form of effective rebellion in and of itself, I also believe that we must take both sides into consideration to move forward. Just as Micale warns against dogmatic readings of hysteria's past, so I warn against unequivocal interpretations of the use of madness in literature. Feminist literary criticism now suffers rather than gains from the polarization of internalist, intellectual approaches—such as French feminist criticism—on the one hand and externalist, sociological approaches such as American Feminism on the other. This polarization accompanied by ideological antagonism has given rise to largely futile disputes motivated less by shared feminist goals than by ego. Myth provides us with a path forward, as it draws attention to the communicative network, social institutions, and political and economic structures through which ideologies are produced and disseminated and thus avoids the formalism and subjectivism of some literary theory, which attempts to extrapolate without any account of the relationship between the two.

To move feminist literary criticism forwards, therefore, I argue for an activated response to the consistent call for a focus on the literary madwoman, on her resolution, and on the narratives that could act for her possible resolution (or emancipation). Yet I also argue for embracing both sides of the madness-as-rebellion controversy and, most importantly, for activating this knowledge in a way that can light a path to effective rebellion for criticism and our culture. In this, I agree with Showalter's quote, which opened Chapter 2, that Hysteria might be claimed as the *first step* on the road to feminism; yet, I would argue, it is only the first step. Situating a protagonist within a broader theorization of structure, myth, and agency offers a productive basis for addressing the category of the literary madwoman subject from the standpoint of feminism, allowing for an incorporation of the work carried out by feminists in psychoanalysis, while at the same time acknowledging the autonomous influence of other social and ideological processes. I believe that this analysis of the literary madwoman, and the ultimate determination of how she can be resolved, is crucial for an emancipatory feminist politics. By enacting feminists' call for revisiting myth, and using this framework to create a narrative analysis that re-visions Herndl's madness as metaphor, we might be able to resolve Caminero-Santaneglo's literary madwoman and move feminist literary criticism beyond the first step.

Notes

1   For a selection, see Luma Balaa, "Why Insanity Is Not Subversive in Hanan Al-Shaykh's Short Story 'Season of Madness'"; Nina Baym "The Madwoman and Her Languages"; Susan K. Cahn, "Border Disorders"; Marta Caminero-Santangelo, *The Madwoman Can't Speak: Or Why Insanity Is Not Subversive*; Phyllis Chesler, *Women and Madness*; Elizabeth J. Donaldson, "The Corpus of the Madwoman"; Shoshana Felman, "Women and Madness: The Critical Phallacy"; Rita Felski, *Beyond Feminist Aesthetics*; Merri Lisa Johnson, *Girl in Need of a Tourniquet: Memoir of a Borderline Personality*; and Elaine Showalter, *The Female Malady: Women, Madness and the English Culture* 1830–1980.

2   See for example Bill Hughes and Kevin Patterson, "The Social Model of Disability and the Disappearing Body: Towards a sociology of impairment"; Tom Shakespeare, *Disability Rights and Wrongs*; Tom Shakespeare and Nicholas Watson, "The social model of disability: An outdated ideology?".

3

Myth and the literary madwoman

Certain myths reveal a great deal about the origins and models of
contemporary female personality. I draw upon them often, as I
describe the relationship between the female condition and what we
call madness—that divinely menacing behavior from whose
eloquence and exhausting demands society protects itself through
"reason" and force. —Phyllis Chesler (55)

The feminist division between approaches to madness in
literature can in many ways be linked to each side's beliefs
about narrative structure. If chaos and irrationality in
fiction are "female" and subversive, they can be rebellious only
when we assume that their opposites, narrative structure and
rationality, are essentially "masculine" and oppressive. Such
approaches are representative of a more general opposition of
masculine symbolic systems and a feminine structure, typifying
what Felski describes as certain trends in feminist poststructuralist thought that "assume that the disintegration of reason
and of symbolic coherence is a liberating cultural phenomenon

emblematic of modernity, a phenomenon that is to be unconditionally affirmed as favourable to the interests of women"
(*Beyond Feminist Aesthetics*, 69). Like Felski, I argue that feminist
theory cannot proceed by assuming that the demise of subjectivity,
truth, and reason are events to be hoped for and uncritically
acclaimed.

This approach to structure has inhibited responses to American
feminist criticism's call for a return to myth, and reflects the
feminist poststructuralist thought that feminine structure is
defined as the *absence* of structure. In many ways, the deconstructionist point of view in French feminist criticism bundles
together terms such as myth, structuralism, and narratology.
Since these terms, and their historical relationship, are vital for
the potential of madness in literature to signify liberation, I
believe that it is also important to explore how the three
approaches to literature converge and diverge (something that
has not yet been done by other writers) and to ask whether by
promoting "myth" as feminist tool we are also espousing a focus
on structuralism.

Although I argue for the possibilities of myth, and that
structured storytelling is humanistic and universal rather than
gendered, I do not subscribe to the belief that every story is really
the same old story—that millennia of fables, myths, folktales,
epics, novels, dramas, novellas, and short stories are nothing
more than "minor variants of one master plot with a single,
prescribed meaning and politics" (Felski, *Beyond Feminist
Aesthetics*, 105). Although I hypothesize that the monomyth's
cyclical structure can be beneficial to feminist literary criticism,
I also argue that the different narrative plot points along the arc
can differ between models, and also between novels.

It is important to note that, while this book focuses on gender
and its impact on narrative structure, gender is only one of many
determining influences upon a female protagonist, with others

ranging from macrostructures (such as class, nationality, and race) down to microstructures (such as the accidents of personal history), which do not simply exist alongside gender distinctions but actively influence and are influenced by them. Yet, as all academics writing books must, I have had to balance the limitations of depth versus breadth within a single work, and have chosen to preference the depth of the discussion over the breadth of the factors considered. It is my hope that other academics who specialize in other fields of feminism, or even feminist literary criticism—such as those in areas considering race and class—can add to this study by increasing the breadth of its application. What I *have* attempted to do, is apply an interdisciplinary approach to allow for the possibility of change rather than simply analysing patterns of gender in narrative structure.

It should also be explained that it is not my intent to provide a thorough history or explanation of structuralism and myth criticism. Structuralism as a school of thought is so complex, and the range of philosophies within it so diverse, that it would be impossible to provide an adequate recapitulation within the confines of this chapter. Nor is it my intent to make light of the contribution of structuralism or myth criticism by simplifying their core concepts. In fact, the approach I take to structuralism and myth criticism is similar to that of the structuralists themselves who, when reading a text or group of texts, as Robert Scholes explains, "give up our general sense of all observable information in exchange for a heightened sense of some specific items" (41), emphasizing some features at the expense of others. Scholes, in his seminal *Structuralism in Literature: An Introduction* (1974), argues that this method provides us with greater conceptual power; that what is lost in mass is gained in energy. I believe this selective approach will best generate the energy required to uncover options for the literary madwoman's resolution.

The monomyth

The concept of the monomyth is drawn from mythography, most famously from Joseph Campbell's model of the hero's journey in *The Hero With a Thousand Faces* (1949). According to Campbell, a myth is a story that coordinates the living person (hero) with the cycle of his/her own life, with the environment in which he or she is living, and with the society that itself has already been integrated into the environment. It is a common belief that not only are myths symbolic representations of our psyches, but also that the role of the hero in myth is universal and that myths help to "instruct individuals in charting a course for their own lives" (*The Hero with a Thousand Faces*, 255). This view is based on the work of Carl Jung—a point explored later in this book—who believed that myth is the symbolic expression given to the unconscious desires, fears, and tensions that underlie the conscious patterns of human behaviour. Therefore, understanding myth puts us in touch with the deep forces that have shaped humanity's destiny and, Campbell argues, "continue to determine both our private and our public lives" (*The Hero with a Thousand Faces,* 256).

For centuries, writers have looked to mythology in an attempt to construct stories that transform their characters' individual experience to one that is universal. It is likely that the concept of a universal narrative appeals to a writer's desire to elicit an emotional response from her readers. Although Campbell and myth criticism has been attacked for "oversimplification and ahistoricism" (Keller, 54), "freeze-dried reductionism" and "logocentric oneness" (Doty, 146), his approach remains popular—there seems to be something about Campbell's philosophy that ignites the imaginations of writers, sociolinguists, anthropologists, psychologists, and critics alike. This influence seems to transcend Campbell's basic structure. For, when scrutinized in terms not of what it is but of how it functions, of how it has served humankind in the past, and of how it may serve today, mythology shows itself to be amenable to the obsessions and requirements of not only feminism but the individual, the race, and the age.

The standard path of the mythological adventure of the hero is a magnification of the formula represented by the process—separation, initiation, return—which might be named the nuclear unit of the monomyth. A hero ventures forth from the world of the commonplace into a realm of supernatural wonder; fabulous forces are there encountered and a decisive victory is won; the hero comes back from this mysterious adventure with the power to bestow boons on his fellow people. The function of this quest narrative, Campbell argues, is to provide a pedagogical structure through which people can learn how best to live a human life.

If fiction should be, as Jonathan Gottschall has recently argued, "the counterforce to social disorder, the tendency of things to fall apart" (138), we can see why writers might find myth's pedagogical function appealing. If French feminist theory has celebrated chaos, madness, and the non-rational, and American feminist theory argues that this approach is not rebellious but in fact supports a character's resignation to extant power systems, then literature utilizing myth's pedagogical function is a way to combat the chaos. Myth offers a potential response to Caminero-Santangelo's and Chesler's desire to privilege forms of agency and illuminate the value of survival.

Analysing Campbell's hero, feminist theorist Pearson notes that, although Campbell initially declares that the hero can be of either gender, he "then proceeds to discuss the heroic pattern as male" and to "define the female characters as goddesses, temptresses and earth mothers" (*The Hero with a Thousand Faces*, 4). Yet the depth of the confused gender depictions of Campbell's heroic outline seems deeper than this statement might suggest.

Campbell's use of gender-inclusive language is conscious and deliberate and, as Robert Segal points out, in illustrating the journey he enlists myths of female heroes as often as those of male ones. Yet, ultimately in the hero's journey the women are the manifestation of evil and the embodiment of desire—where man is self/agent, she is his undifferentiated all/other. At the heart of the journey, woman recalled to nature becomes symbolic flesh: sex, desire, generative motherhood. As flesh, woman loses her agency and it is the male who retains it, and with it the ability to act as hero. Woman disappears and is replaced by symbol because she is not fully allowed her subjectivity.

The heroine's journey

A number of publications have proposed feminine variations of the hero's journey. Murdock's *The Heroine's Journey* (1990), Hudson's *The Virgin's Promise* (2009) and Frankel's *From Girl to Goddess: The Heroine's Journey Through Myth and Legend* (2010) argue that a careful examination of the central agent of the hero's journey finds that the subject, protagonist, and central individual of each articulation is consistently "man." While Campbell suggests that "the whole sense of the ubiquitous myth of the hero's passage is that it shall serve as a general pattern for men and women" (*The Hero with a Thousand Faces*, 121), a point subscribed to by Christopher Vogler in his rewriting of Campbell's work for screenwriters, these writers suggest that when analyzing the journey's zenith or central point, the hero is distinctly male. It is the woman who serves as a crisis at the nadir of the male hero's journey and, in mythic symbology, Campbell argues that woman represents the totality of what can be known for the hero. Murdock questioned Campbell about the difference between the female and male journey in 1981 and was deeply unsatisfied by his response. During their discussion, Campbell suggested that women "don't need to make the journey" and that "in the whole of mythological tradition the woman is there ... all she has to do is realize that she's the place that people are trying to get to" (Murdock, 2).

While all the abovementioned feminist mythologists espouse a heroine's journey that differs from that of the hero, Frankel's almost mirrors Campbell's monomyth. This might be due to the texts from which Frankel drew her inspiration. Campbell and Frankel take their picture of the monomythic cycle from wide-ranging historic sources: Greek, Roman, Persian, Melanesian, Korean, Celtic, and Egyptian myths; the Bible; Jewish, Buddhist, and Hindu texts; the Quran; shamanic Siberian tales; and James Joyce, and Shakespeare. The two mythologists loosen the boundaries between religious text, sacred recollection, mythology, literature, and folklore, and they pose the journey as hermeneutic—in both psychoanalytic and spiritual terms, a journey of self. Yet they both look to historic texts to form their journeys.

Murdock and Hudson also utilize historic texts as the basis for their models but, in contrast, adapt their journeys to encompass a contemporary perspective. For Murdock, these are the stories of women she has heard in her practice as a psychologist. For twenty-five years prior to writing her text, Murdock had heard a resounding cry of dissatisfaction from women who have embraced the hero's journey. These personal stories motivated Murdock to write *The Heroine's Journey.*

Murdock proposes that a woman's quest is to become a "fully integrated, balanced, and whole human being and to heal the deep wound of the feminine" (3). First, we embrace the masculine principles ruling society, often rejecting our female natures, which we are taught to see as powerless. We join the "heroic" journey with male allies and role models. Later in life, we are unsatisfied with the world's definition of success. We experience a period of dryness and despair, confronting the "dark feminine"—our own feelings of loss and anger. When a woman decides not to play by the patriarchal rules, she has no guidelines to follow. Not knowing the answers, we look to our intuition and become what Murdock calls "spiritual warriors." We seek to heal the mother–daughter split and integrate our female values with our learned masculine skills. It is important to note from the outset that Murdock does not believe that this journey only occurs once; it is a continuous cycle, repeated throughout our lives.

In contrast, Hudson focuses on the unique archetypal path of the "virgin"—that is, the young female or princess character. Both Murdock and Hudson take care to draw parallels between their own work and Campbell's so that the hero's journey is not rejected but acknowledged as part of their larger system. As a result, Murdock's and Hudson's models build upon components of Campbell's theory, while contributing knowledge gained from more recent research and experience.

Yet, there is a clear distinction between the hero's and the heroine's journeys. The narratives' different settings illustrate the internal and external aspects of the process of knowing oneself as an individual, and thus the hero and the heroine symbolize two aspects of knowing one's place in the world. The archetypal journey takes the protagonist from one polarity to the other: from shadow to light. Yet the hero's and heroine's descent to the shadow and the ascent to the light travel in different directions and, in turn, growth initiates from two different origins. The hero begins his journey with a strong sense of self-preservation and ultimately embarks on an externally-focused descent, then ascends to achieve individuation. In contrast, the heroine begins her story lacking a sense of self, giving too much energy to the needs and opinions of others, and embarks upon an internally focused journey of descent from which she travels outward and ascends to achieve her individuation.

For the purposes of this book, a heroine's journey model, which includes an interpretation of the modern-day heroine, has been chosen as it parallels the purposes of feminist literature outlined previously. That is, the heroine's journey focuses on a female as the protagonist, on claiming an "I" for one's story and putting women at the centre of the narrative. Since Hudson focuses solely on the "virgin" character, Maureen Murdock's heroine's journey is a possible feminist narratological framework to conduct a new reading of female madness in literature.

Consequently, the intersection between recent American feminist literary studies and myth criticism points us towards Murdock's heroine's journey as the vehicle to create Caminero-Santangelo's imaginative space—a space in which a female reader can envision herself as an agent for change. With this knowledge, we are able to rephrase Caminero-Santangelo's question of how one symbolically resolves the madwoman in a fictional text to a more specific question: how can Murdock's heroine's journey be used to construct a new narrative that symbolically resolves the madwoman?

To determine how the madwoman could be resolved in literature, I believe we must investigate the narrative structure of the texts central to the argument that madness is an effective form of rebellion. These texts are, I would argue, examples of subjective realism, which are clearly recognisable as modifications of existing genres such as the *Bildungsroman*. Given that realist feminist writing does not, as Felski argues, "comprise unique genres, but rather appropriates and reworks existing literary structures to create distinctive woman-centred narratives," only an approach that links "formal and thematic analysis to a theorization of frameworks of reception can remain sensitive to the historical specificity of feminist literature as a cultural product" (*Beyond Feminist Aesthetics*, 84). The intersection between Chesler's call for mythical structures and Felski's call for historical frameworks points towards a monomyth, specifically Murdock's heroine's journey, as a framework for analysing the literary madwoman and, most importantly, to working towards determining her resolution.

Figure 1: Maureen Murdock's model of the heroine's journey

Thus, this framework is a possible guide to determining the narrative journey of the literary madwoman; where she begins, how she develops, and where she ends. This analysis is crucial to determining how one might resolve the literary madwoman, and is yet to be conducted. I argue for an exploration of the intersection and interrelationships between myth criticism, narratology, psychoanalysis, and feminist literary criticism.

The following analysis of three literary texts determines how and when the texts correlate and deviate from the stages of Murdock's heroine's journey (Figure 1). It also pinpoints, when there is correlation, the specific nature of the similarity and whether these similarities can be witnessed across the three texts. Thus, I conduct both a vertical analysis (comparing the individual texts with the heroine's journey) and a horizontal analysis (comparing these patterns across the three texts). To undertake a comparison of these texts is not to attempt to collapse the differences between them but, rather, to bring to light the common frames of reference on which they rely.

Additionally, while the points along the journey model can easily verge and converge, displaying similarities and differences, the key point along the journey model is at the bottom—that moment of darkness, madness, descent, which all the texts mentioned in this book as containing a "literary madwoman" have in common.

Before continuing, the issue of confirmation bias needs to be addressed. It could be argued that any findings in this chapter and the next, and indeed the later sections of this book, are the result not of rational, objective analysis, but of paying attention to information that confirmed what I believed while ignoring any information that challenged my preconceived notions. In scientific study, there are approaches designed to avoid confirmation bias—primarily the act of anticipating any objections, checking whether those objections are valid and then determining realistic parameters to test and retest findings. Certainly, literary critics such as Jonathan Gottschall would be supportive of this approach and recommend its complete integration with literary studies, so as to forestall any imputation that literary study is not a serious academic practice. Yet studies in the humanities are not studies in science and nor should they be. As soon as one begins to reduce either into the other, one loses the very essence that makes each field so vital.

Also, post-colonial literary critics have criticized the tendency of often white middle-class female critics and theorists to deduce a generalized notion of female experience from their own lives, and both they and Marxist feminists have challenged attempts to produce a distinctive common denominator that unites the experience of all women across historical, class, racial, and national boundaries. This criticism could be aimed squarely at this study; however, rather than attempting to include literature that is not within my field of expertise, or on the other hand succumbing to a fear of making any precise arguments or statements so that my contribution to feminist literary criticism is at best watered down, I can only acknowledge the limitations of a book that does not focus on close readings of diverse literary texts.

What I *do* hope to achieve is a socially and historically contextualized interpretation and contribution since, if a feminist approach to literature is to link the analysis of texts to broader questions of social and cultural change, it must situate literature in relation to the theorization of social processes as they affect the status of women—in the context of this book, the historical and, I would argue, current association of femininity with madness.

By situating texts and characters in context with parallel historical interpretations and theorizations of women's madness, and by interpreting how these approaches intersect and diverge from feminist literary criticism's textual interpretations, it is possible to identify, or at least postulate, links between feminism and literature.

Separation from the feminine

The beginning of the hero's journey is marked by a movement towards a goal, a call to adventure, an expedition in order to achieve a desired result. In contrast, Murdock's heroine's journey begins with a movement *away*, a separation both physically and psychologically from a mother or mother archetype, either by choice or by force. In *The Bell Jar, Wide Sargasso Sea, Surfacing* and *The Woman Upstairs*, the female protagonists experience both a literal and a figurative detachment, which is foreshadowed by criticisms of femininity. Esther in *The Bell Jar* describes herself as separate from the "awfully boring" women in her hotel "waiting to get married to some career man or other." Among the "starched cotton" women who fit into society's expectations for cheerful and flexible women, Esther feels she must repress her natural gloom, cynicism, and dark humour. She is supposed to be having the "time of her life" whirling around the New York fashion world but merely feels empty and numb. Esther's sense of alienation from the world around her comes from the desire to reject the expectations placed upon her as a young woman living in 1950s America.

Antoinette's rejection by her mother in *Wide Sargasso Sea* is foreshadowed by the feminine image of the orchids that are "not to be touched" and that she never goes near. The flower, often said to represent a beautiful lady, is "wonderful to see" but, for Antoinette, it remains "out of reach."

Similarly, before we learn that Atwood's narrator (hereafter referred to simply as Narrator) has lost her mother, she criticizes stereotypically feminine traits. She observes women as being vain (Anna does not wear jeans because she "looks fat in them"), whining (the loggers' wives sit on back porches and complain) or of secondary importance to their husband's priorities (Narrator's mother and Madame endure uncomfortable silences as their husbands enact a pointless tradition of exchange).

In *The Woman Upstairs*, Nora—presumably a reference to Ibsen's Nora in *A Doll's House*—chooses, like Esther, a different life than that that was expected of her mother, who "burned over the consuming demands of motherhood." When choosing between studying art or teaching at university Nora's mother encourages a career that can provide financial stability so that her daughter does not have to become chained to children and husband—"each day more trapped, until she was buried in her aloneness." Nora makes this decision over and over—to study teaching, to take the high-paying management position, to work as a teacher, to again and again choose a safe and stable career so that she not only never becomes her mother but also is never forced to face her true desire and fear of living an artist's life. Her mother teaches her by example—by the "whimsical, panicked procrastination" of her childhood and then, more brutally, by the "prolonged, involuntary shutting-up-shop" of her mother's body—that dreams are "preposterous" and that "fate is a jailer." Interestingly, we see many similarities between Esther, a character created in the sixties, and Nora, a character created in the early twenty-first century. Reading both books, it is easy to ask: although so much has changed, have the expectations, struggles, decisions really changed at all?

In these examples of repeated reproval, we see the protagonists distance themselves from apparently feminine attributes. The mother archetype is often referred to as the unconscious, involving the body and soul; but it is also a symbol, Murdock explains, "for the collective unconscious, which contains the unity of all opposites" (17). In all four narratives, the heroine's separation from the feminine fosters imbalance. As a result, the stories depict confusion, uncertainty, and insecurity. Antoinette is unable to distinguish between her friends and her enemies, her family rejects her, the little girl Tia steals her clothes, and she is betrayed by her husband. Esther also feels out of place and consumed by confusion. She feels anxiety about her future because she can see only mutually exclusive choices: virgin or whore, submissive wife or successful but lonely career woman. In this way, Esther's separation from the mother archetype prevents any integration of, or harmony between, the binaries by which she is taunted.

Narrator is also haunted by the separation of dualities: the body and mind, the natural and the man-made, the truth and imitation. She is, almost literally, in limbo as she travels into what is supposed to be the familiar territory of her hometown but is, in fact, a land transformed by progress. Driving in the car, they are "between stations"; Narrator or her companions are in the "wrong place," and everything seems an imitation: the cherub with the missing face, the moose dressed as humans, Paul and his wife who are "like carvings," and the bar's "regulation picture" that is an imitation of a nineteenth-century shooting lodge. There are also repeated images of physical uncertainty. Once at her childhood lodge, she repeatedly sees visions of severed heads or limbs; she often fears that her body could fall apart or lose an arm, like Madame in the old store. She describes divorce (which we later realize is an abortion) as an amputation and is sure that she could have amnesia and no one would notice.

Similarly, Nora is constantly at odds with herself, wearing a mask for the outside world and severing herself from her art. She realizes later that this detachment was caused by fear, and that her fear was in fact her mother's fear; that she had shouldered all her mother's anxieties and disappointments. Yet, interestingly, even once she realizes this Nora does not, in fact, pursue her art for arts sake, or even for her sake, but for the sake of an unattainable and unrequited form of love(s).

Although the heroine's journey depicts a variety of ways in which a woman may separate from her mother, including the choice to reject her parent, the four novels describe protagonists who are abandoned by their mothers. Antoinette's mother's rejection is physical and emotional: "she pushed me away, not roughly but calmly, coldly, without a word, as if she had decided once and for all that I was useless to her." One evening her mother does not speak to her or look at her at all, and Antoinette takes this as a sign that her mother is "ashamed of her." That night, the little girl dreams she is walking in a forest but not alone. Someone who hates her is there, but out of sight. She hears heavy footsteps coming closer and closer to her, but even though she struggles and screams she is unable to move. She wakes to find her mother looking down at her. Antoinette may be "safe from strangers" but she repeatedly describes feeling frightened of her mother. In the morning, she wakes knowing that "nothing would be the same," that it would "change and go on changing." Murdock describes this process as "particularly intense" and explains that the daughter will experience a fear of loss, anxiety about being alone, separate, and difficult because she must differentiate herself from someone who was "the same as her" (19). After her nightmare, Antoinette runs away, visiting parts of Coulibri she has never seen, where there is no road, path or track. Interestingly, we see this image mirrored in *Surfacing*, where Narrator thought she knew the way home but has to ask for directions because the old road is closed.

During her wandering, Antoinette realizes that it is as if a door has opened and she is "somewhere else, something else, someone else." Here, we see the daughter's geographical and physical separation from her mother and the sadness that comes with the movement from the fused symbiotic relationship of mother and daughter to separateness and, in turn, a new identity. Antoinette's experience of her mother as absent and unable to mother her encourages the relationship she develops with Christophine as she sets out to find "an older," more "positive female role model."

Similarly, Esther's mother in *The Bell Jar*, Mrs Greenwood, is depicted as unfeeling and is never shown displaying any warmth or emotion towards her daughter. Mrs Greenwood is a practical woman and stresses the need for Esther to have skills such as shorthand; even the "apostles were tent makers," she argues. This focus on the practical frustrates Esther and she defines her mother as a martyr who sacrificed her own life after her husband died; like Antoinette with Christophine, Esther embraces an alternative mother figure, in this case Jay Cee: "I wish I had a mother like Jay Cee. Then I'd know what to do." Esther feels her mother is useless to her: "My own mother wasn't much help." As she sits on the *Ladies' Day* banquet table, she muses on what a long way she has come—a long way from her mother's suffocating encouragement to "settle" just has she had done, and a long way from Mrs Willard, her boyfriend's mother, who sacrificed her career for her husband and children, and whom she sees as an equivalent to her mother. This self-sacrifice can be seen in the description of Mrs Greenwood's hands after Esther's first treatment: "bone white, as if the skin had worn off them in the hour of waiting." Certainly, Mrs Greenwood has been eternally waiting, passively accepting and experiencing the tragedies in her life, gliding from one place to the other with Esther, without leaving and without arriving.

Narrator describes her mother in a similar fashion. When visiting her mother in hospital, Narrator describes her as a "harsh bird" with "clinging claws" and "absent eyes." At one point, Narrator decides that her mother's lack of personal interest might mean her mother does not even know who she, Narrator, is. Leaving the hospital, Narrator steals her mother's journal in the hope that it will include something about her. Yet all it contains is seasonal commentary: "no emotions, no reflections." In this way, like Esther's mother, the protagonist's mother emotionally rejects her daughter and refuses to engage in anything that could be defined as personal inquiry. Narrator not only rejects the feminine, as the other characters do; she also rejects becoming a mother herself. Whether in the beginning, when we believe she has abandoned her baby, or towards the end, when we realize she was encouraged to have an abortion, Narrator is not only rejected by her own mother but herself rejects motherhood.

Again, in a protagonist depicted over thirty years later, Nora has a similar experience. Her mother, "fierce and strange and doomed" repeatedly enters "darker phases" that push Nora away. In fact, her mother, towards the end of her life, says to Nora: "Life's funny. You have to find a way to keep going, to keep laughing, even after you realize that none of your dreams will come true." In this statement, Nora not only hears that having dreams is pointless, but that she was not enough for her mother; that Nora was not, in any way, a dream come true for her mother.

The portrayal of mothers in the three texts reiterates the daughter-centric narrative approach, in which mothers are prevented from voicing their own story and are constrained within what Elizabeth Podnieks describes as the "age-old dichotomies" (4) of the angel or the whore—they remain demonized characters. Even in *Surfacing,* Narrator is critical both of the decisions she has made as a potential mother and of her mother. When we leave Narrator at the end of the text, in a state of supposed pregnancy, she is confined to a private life, unable to move forward into the public sphere. All the protagonists are highly critical of their mothers, even when, towards the end of the novels, they have gained more understanding and what could therefore be expected to manifest greater empathy.

Identification with the masculine

Their separation from their mothers causes all four characters—Antoinette, Esther, Narrator and Nora—to reject the feminine and search for recognition by the "father," literally and/or figuratively. Since "men are in a position of strength ... women look to men for support to strengthen themselves" (Murdock, 27). It is interesting that once Antoinette has been rejected by her mother and begins to identify with the masculine, the narrative's point of view changes from Antoinette's to that of her husband. Antoinette's mother's failings, internalized as part of the inner negative mother, cause her to feel humiliated about being female and, therefore, unworthy of a point of view. It is the masculine that must speak—the strong, the patriarchal. However, a positive masculine role model was as absent from Antoinette's life as her mother's affection. Both her father and feelings of safety, as if they were connected in some way, "belong to the past." Her only other male role model is her stepfather, Mr Cosway, who promises Antoinette and her fortune to an Englishman. Once she is married, Antoinette—after a short hesitation—puts her life in his hands: "I never wished to live before I knew you. I always thought it would be better if I died." Antoinette's husband now has all the power—it is his voice, his point of view. He has control over her finances, her estate and her happiness: "suppose you took this happiness away when I wasn't looking." The damaging effect of Antoinette's absent father means that she believes she does not exist except in the mirror of male attention.

Esther's father is also a figure of the past, resented by Mrs Greenwood for dying and leaving them with nothing. Esther, having rejected the feminine and living a life devoid of positive male role models, seeks approval and encouragement from the masculine world of scholarships, success at college, writing prizes and work experience in New York. In Esther, we see Murdock's description of the inner masculine figure as "not a man with a heart but a greedy tyrant that never lets up ... nothing is ever enough"; he "drives her forward, more, better, faster, with no recognition of her longings to be loved, to feel satisfied, or even to rest" (39). Esther was supposed to be having "the time of her life"; people see her "steering New York like her own private car." But she admits to herself, and the reader, that she is not steering anything, not even herself. This is because her inner masculine figure has the wheel and is controlling her journey. But, on and on, she tries to convince herself:

> All my life I'd told myself studying and writing and working like mad was what I wanted to do, and it actually seemed to be true, I did everything well enough and got all As, and by the time I made it to college nobody could stop me. (33)

When Esther meets Constantine, he fills the void left by the missing father figure. She hopes he will see through her bravado, to who she really is, and when he squeezes her hand she feels happy—happier than she has been since "running along the hot white beaches with her father." Esther realizes at this point that she has never been happy since that time.

The search for a father is also Narrator's driving force in *Surfacing*, yet, in her case, she is looking for her actual father who has "simply disappeared ... vanished into nothing," rather than a replacement figure. Even before her father goes missing, she aligns herself more with a masculine than feminine image. When she first meets Joe, he falls for her "coolness" after they have sex, by the way she "puts on her clothes ... as if she is feeling no emotion." She also takes on the masculine role at her childhood lodge, as she catches frogs in jars, hooks them on lines and kills fish: "this was never my job, someone else did it, my brother or father." It is clear that the "someone else" is a masculine other.

Nora has a strained relationship with her father and struggles to have any real conversation with him; in many ways she searches for the connection and attention that she does not receive from her parents through other relationships and, at the same time, seeks their approval through her career decisions. Even her dream of becoming an artist is, in many ways, motivated by her teacher's approval of her, the "flicker of glee" that comes to his face when he sees her art, his exclamation that, this, "now this is a work of art"; "Well done, you," he says, and at once we can imagine the teenage girl feeling approved of by and enough for Mr Crace. Later, when she is offered a high-paid and respected job with a management consultancy, Nora is still consumed by the need for approval: "once something like that was offered, how could I say no?" She barely looks at art, thinking her plan to become an artist "had been a fantasy of the powerless" and that, with money of her own, "with power" of her own, she has "no need of it." This need for power, security, prestige, haunts Nora throughout her journey.

Antoinette, Esther, Narrator, and Nora find temporary comfort in the masculine world—in the prevailing myth in our culture that certain people (husbands, professionally successful men, fathers), positions (employers such as Jay Cee and Nora's management consultancy) and events (marriage and scholarships) possess more inherent value than others (Murdock, 29). Although in the heroine's journey there is an archetype of the father as ally, the madwoman as heroine in these four novels seeks to be valued either by becoming like men and/or becoming liked by men.

Road of trials: meeting ogres and dragons

The outer road of trials takes Antoinette, Esther, Narrator, and Nora through the expected obstacle courses that lead them through education, employment, marriage, promotions, prestigious titles, and financial success. Along the way, these women face ogres, dragons, and monsters resembling boyfriends, parents, friends, and employers who tell them they cannot possibly succeed.

Antoinette's dragon is not only her husband, but also the temptation of sex, care, and dependency disguised as requirements for love, power and achievement. Her husband's[1] physical interest ("I did not love her.... I was thirsty for her"); his protection ("'You are safe', I'd say.... She'd liked that—to be told you are safe"); and his need to be pleased and taken care of ("You must let me cover you up," "I'll wear the dress you like tonight ... and I will have another made exactly like it ... will you be pleased?") flatter Antoinette into thinking she has arrived in a place of power and independence, when in fact all she has received are the "talismans of success" (Murdock, 48).

Esther's primary ogre is Buddy Willard and the illusions he provides. Buddy makes Esther feel sexy and experienced. He improves her credibility with older students and changes her view of herself from someone who is set up on blind dates with "pale mushroomy men" with "protruding ears or buck teeth or a bad leg," to a woman who has earned the attention of a handsome Yale medical student. Buddy represents the ideal 1950s American male and subscribes, like Mrs Greenwood, to society's notions about and expectations of women. Because Esther takes everything Buddy says as the "honest-to-God truth," his criticism of Esther's interest in poetry and his unapologetic sexual conduct with a waitress undermine her clarity, self-confidence, and self-worth. When Esther realizes that she has not been happy since her father died, she begins to add up all the things she cannot do. But these are not just talents she lacks, they are feminine traits she believes she does not possess. Esther begins with cooking, which her grandmother and mother could do, then moves on to shorthand, which her mother teaches and has been encouraging her to learn. The list grows longer and longer until she feels completely inadequate. Without a positive male role model in her life she has never developed the self-confidence to be able to battle with the dragons and ogres that now rage within and around her.

Narrator is also taunted by internal and external ogres. Her internal dragon prefers logic and the mind, and she finds herself caught up trying to decipher her father's codes. Yet she is really "covering over the bad things and filling empty spaces with an embroidery of calculations and numbers." There is no room for dreams, love, or emotions. For a while she wanted to become an artist, but her ex-partner convinces her that there have "never been any important women artists" and that she should study design. Like Antoinette and Esther, Narrator believes everything her ex-partner says and discards her own feelings to accommodate his beliefs.

Similarly, Nora when she first meets Skandar doesn't trust him; she dreams of having sex with him and then he having a "sly far-away smile" with "just a glint of tooth." Yet, even though she feels this unease, she places her self-worth almost completely in his hands and believes everything he says. It is not just desire that she feels for Sirena, Skandar and Reza but longing; "longing is a better word than desire," she explains, "it's a quality of reaching but not attaining, of yearning, of a physical pull that is so intense and yet melancholy, always already so sorrowful, self-knowing, in some wise passionate and in some measure resigned." Nora places her entire emotional wellbeing in their hands; when they go away she is bereft; she waits at the phone, she imagines why they have not contacted her, she tells Skandar of her hunger for life not to share her truth with him, but in anticipation of his response. Each of these characters, in his or her own way, becomes Nora's compass; the "impassioned interior conversations" she has with them grants her some aspect of her most "dearly held, most fiercely hidden, heart's desires: life, art, motherhood, love" and, like the other protagonists, the "great seductive promise that I wasn't nothing." Of course, the final revelation, Nora's viewing of her private pleasure as a video in Sirena's exhibition, is the ultimate betrayal.

Rochester, Buddy, Narrator's ex-partner, and the Shahids are the gatekeepers of the women's self-confidence, self-definition, reality, and truth. All are similar in their behaviour and treatment of Antoinette, Esther, Narrator and Nora. All cheat on their partners; undermine the women's passions—for a West Indies home, for poetry, for art, for company and connectedness; and use sex and desire as a way to manipulate and overpower. In all four novels, the male characters (and, for Nora, Sirena as well, though like the male characters she is a love interest) can also be seen as individual representations of a wider patriarchal society or context—Rochester and the English; Buddy and 1950s America; Narrator's ex-partner and the "Americans"; the Shahids, the three "blank monks" who prophesize and promise but then abandon. With self-righteous and self-interested expectations, all these ogres and dragons prevent the women from trusting their own sense of the truth. Rather than forming a stage in the journey, as Murdock represents it, the road of trials —meeting ogres and dragons—seems to occur throughout the novels.

The boon of success

Antoinette, Esther, Narrator, and Nora become enamoured with the accolades that "winning" brings. There is a great adrenaline rush associated with the achievement of a goal, and this masks the deep-seated pain associated with not being enough as a person. This sense of not being enough has been created by their relationships with their mothers, and by their mothers' own internal relationship with herself. As in Murdock's explanation of this stage, none of the protagonists' mothers could express their loneliness, "their abandonment, their sense of loss directly" (Murdock, 64). This repression, in Esther's, Antoinette's,

Narrator's, and Nora's mothers, meant that all they could express was criticism, anger and, sometimes, even rage. This behaviour, Murdock argues, forces the protagonists to question: doesn't my mother like being a woman, having a husband, being a mother? Did children ruin her life? Was being a woman awful? Would her life be ruined because she was female? Their mothers' self-denigration and self-hate, Murdock argues, in turn convinced Esther, Antoinette, Narrator, and Nora to fear being anything like their mothers and therefore to try their hardest to be the exact opposite. Yet this constant searching for an identity in opposition to that of their mothers leads the protagonists to develop a warped perception of success. Their constructs of "success" are deeply flawed: Antoinette believes that if she can make her husband want her, to desire her physically, then she will be happy; Esther believes that if she can have sex with someone other than Buddy, she will achieve some sort of retribution for his affair. The rewards of the outer journey are seductive and the protagonists are unable to sacrifice the false notions of the heroic to find the "inner" boons of success. Antoinette, Esther, Narrator and Nora are each unable to achieve two main things at this stage: autonomy and detachment from ego.

This focus on the ego and the establishment of identity in the outer world—Esther as a "writer," Antoinette as a "wife," Narrator as an "artist," and Nora also as an "artist" but then again also as being "loved" by the Shahids—has made them independent, self-sufficient, and motivated by the desire to not rely on anyone. The protagonists drive others away or drive themselves away from others. This retreat is, in many ways, motivated by their misconceptions of what success as a person, a woman, a wife, a writer, an artist, someone who is loved, wanted and seen, looks like.

None of these heroines can discard their old ideas of success. Antoinette, Esther, Narrator, and Nora all fall into sexually destructive cycles because they believe the act of sex will bring them what they need. For Antoinette, this is love; for Esther, independence; for Narrator, a baby; and for Nora, to be truly seen. In addition, the heroines are unable to find the courage to realize that they are adequate just as they are. They are unable to detach themselves from the whims of the ego and say, "I am not all things ... and I am enough" (Murdock, 68). Antoinette, Esther, Narrator, and Nora are trapped by an attachment to their egos. Therefore, the madwoman as heroine, rather than finding the inner boon of success, succumbs to the outer temptations of her ego.

Awakening to feelings of spiritual aridity: death

When Antoinette's husband stops giving her attention, she seeks Christophine's advice: "He does not love me, I think he hates me. He always sleeps in his dressing room ... if I get angry he is scornful ... I cannot endure it anymore." Antoinette believes that if Christophine can use *obeah*[2] to make her husband come to her one more night, she could make him love her. But when Christophine tells her she cannot make him love her, Antoinette says she does not care, she just wants him to want her for one more night. Antoinette is so constantly afraid that she begins to sink into a state of depression. This forces her to betray Christophine and, in this section of the novel, Antoinette is narrator once more. Antoinette gives her husband the potion and they make love; but, the next day, he has an affair with Amélie right next door to his wife. Yet it is the fact that her husband has destroyed her beloved home that hurts her the most. Antoinette smashes a bottle and, "with broken glass in her hand and murder in her eyes," she calls her husband a coward and becomes red-eyed and wild-haired.

Esther begins to feel like a champion college footballer suddenly confronted by Wall Street and a business suit—his days of glory shrunk to a little gold cup on his mantle with a date engraved on it, like the date on a tombstone. Like the footballer, Esther believes her glory days are over. In trying to be everything to everyone, in her constant desire for recognition and success, she has become over-worked, confused, and depressed. She describes herself as sitting in the crotch of a fig tree with lots of figs hanging in the tree above her: a happy family, a famous poet, a brilliant professor. She wants them all and, because she cannot choose just one, the figs all shrivel up and fall to the ground at her feet.

When Narrator realizes that her memory is playing tricks on her and that she was never married, that she was having an affair with a married man that led to a pregnancy and an abortion, she believes she has failed, that she is "inoculated, exempt, classified as wounded." It is at this point the reader can revisit her memories and interpret them with new knowledge. When she describes the divorce as like an amputation—"you survive but there is less of you"—we realize she is actually describing the abortion and that, as a result of losing the baby, she feels like less of a person. It is this event that marks the "funny break" Anna reads from her hand and she becomes dislocated from her heart and her body. She has been "split in two," dislocated from the ability to feel physically or emotionally: a "woman sawn apart in a wooden crate ... a trick done with mirrors ... only with me there had been an accident and I came apart. The other half, the one locked away, was the only one that could live; I was the wrong half, detached, terminal. I was nothing but a head." And so we see Narrator becoming the madwoman in her attic. It is now not her father's death she is worried about but her own, though not a future death but one from the past—the "break" referred to in her life line, the time of the abortion, during which she distanced herself from any emotion.

Another split is that between Nora's made-up world and her

reality. For several months (and, Nora realizes, probably several years), her "state of fantasy," the country to which she "largely decamped," was where she "preferred to stay." Yet, slowly, doubt creeps into this fantasy world and light is shone on the dark denial Nora has hidden from herself: "I believed them. I built houses, and entire lives, upon those beliefs. If you'd told me my own story about someone else, I would have assured you that this person was completely unhinged." One trigger of this doubt is the Shahid's move back to Paris, when Nora is forced to face her reality, her loneliness, the real state of her life. Women Upstairs, Nora explains, must never think of themselves—*never*, she stresses—as alone, forlorn or, God help us, wanting. It will not do. It cannot be. "It is the end." And, indeed, this martyrdom, when the Shahids leave her life after making her feel as though she was so necessary, so needed by them, starts a cascade of emotion; when Nora starts to play victim in her mind, it is the beginning of the end for her: "I felt forsaken by hope. I felt like I'd been seen clearly, and discarded, dropped back into the undiscriminated pile like a shell upon the shore." Once Nora feels, not only a sense of isolation, but a sense of truth about how the Shahids really feel about her, she describes the result as a kind of death. In being the one that was left behind, the one who is far removed from the family going on with their lives, happy, without her, "it was as if I was dying, rather than they. I was the one who had to give them up, and in so doing, give up the world."

Descent to the goddess

Most important is to understand the narrative closure, or end of descent, of the madwoman's journey and, in turn, the ways in which madness is used as narrative closure. During the heroine's descent in Murdock's model, she experiences a period of introversion and depression, a slow painful process through which her identity is scraped away. This descent into darkness is represented in all four novels: Antoinette is a prisoner in an English attic, Esther believes she is confined in the stale air of a bell jar, Narrator identifies with trapped animals and babies in jars, and Nora believes she has been "packed up" with the Shahid's blankets and books.

As Rochester begins to rename Antoinette as Bertha, she becomes lost in the dark and wishes to stay there, "where she belongs." She feels an incredible sense of emptiness and goes back to a state of body/mind before there were words. Antoinette has "looked for love in all the wrong places" and it has broken her (Murdock, 107). In the attic in England, we see Antoinette in a cold, dark cave where her identity is finally eradicated: "There is no looking glass here and I do not know what I am like now." Antoinette is a ghost of herself.

Esther also loses herself towards the end of *The Bell Jar*. She "practices her new, normal personality" on Irwin, behaviour she needs to exercise since it has come from the shock therapy rather than from any real personal insight. Yet we also see that, behind the changed façade, Esther is still battling the same demons. Esther decides to seduce Irwin to spite Buddy—who slept with a waitress over summer—and only after she has seen his study, the room of a mathematician. Her inner masculine still controls her decisions and she remains driven by the need to "measure up and achieve according to male-defined standards" (Murdock, 74). Esther lies about where she is staying to Doctor Nolan and so is caught up in the same tricks. When Esther feels the blood between her legs, the "tradition" she feels a part of—the blood-stained bridal sheets, the capsules of red ink bestowed upon already deflowered brides—is not part of a feminine tradition, it is part of a line of practices designed to conform to male expectations. Esther is no more aware of the continuing influence of masculine forces in determining how she behaves than she was at the beginning of the novel, when she believed everything

Buddy told her. Yet, when Esther haemorrhages after losing her virginity, she is "fixed" by a male doctor at the hospital, just as she is shocked into recovery in the asylum. With her emotions buried and her life force stopped, Esther loses an element of her truth, her ability to see the whole picture since part of it is always buried: the ugly, the crazy, the denied, the disappeared.

Narrator marks her descent by staying at her childhood lodge while her companions return to the mainland, since to leave with them would be running away and "the truth is here." She turns the mirror around so it "no longer traps me"—a gesture similar to that of Antoinette—removes her clothes in an animalistic gesture and dons the blanket her mother used to wear when she experienced bouts of depression. Narrator begins to shed her human identity, yet she is also terrified of losing control, of letting go of the logic she has held on to like a crutch: "Blank dark, I can see nothing.... The fear arrives like waves ... it's my skin that is afraid, rigid ... that they should arrive is logical; but logic is a wall, I built it, on the other side is terror." She tries to inflict rules on her descent—a focus on the mind, just as Esther focuses on the mathematician and getting back at Buddy—but the rules continually change.

Similarly, towards the end of *The Woman Upstairs* Nora lies awake with her aging relatives, "stock still, eyes open, waiting for dawn, seized in an unmasterable panic at the loss of my so-beloved, apparently unreal life." Not only has she lost the family with which she fell in love, but their requital of this love is also questioned; indeed, her belief of their reciprocation falls apart as she falls apart. This realization also brings with it realization of other truths that Nora has been denying, such as other people's opinions of her—their pity of her relationship status and patronizing compliments about her work ethic and talent with children —"all of this you know," she explains, you "bury them deep, like dead men, but they're there, the skeletons are there, and you're always with them."

All four women make lists in their heads of their histories, their pasts. Antoinette remembers "the grandfather clock ... Aunt Cora's patchwork ... orchids ... her doll's house and her mother's parrot." Esther remembers "the cadavers ... and Doreen ... the story of the fig-tree and Marco's diamond ... the broken thermometers ... the rock that bulged between sky and sea." Narrator reads through her childhood scrapbook, burns her attempts at drawing princesses and discards her fake wedding ring in an attempt to eliminate everything from the past. Nora lists the imaginary past beliefs—"our friendships, my loves, these people, my inventions."

Yet, as Esther remarks, it is not about forgetting the past, covering it up like a kind of snow; it is about acknowledging the landscape of the self. Ultimately, though, the protagonists in all four texts repress their pasts and are unable to acknowledge their personal feelings or opinions. In this way, we witness the separation from subjectivity discussed in the previous chapter.

The descent can, as Murdock explains, often be precipitated by a life-changing loss. Antoinette loses her culture and her home and, even before she is taken to England, she believes her husband has ruined the West Indies for her. Esther loses her place in the writing workshop and, therefore, a large part of her identity; Narrator loses her baby after being coerced into having an abortion, and also loses her father; and Nora loses what she believed to be the loves of her life and then, with the showing of the video, also her dignity. Murdock explains that this bereavement can open the space for "dismemberment and descent" (88).

Women need to find themselves, Murdock explains, not by "moving up and into the light like men"—such as in Esther's rise up to sit on the doctor's table, or her entrance and acceptance into the asylum meeting room—but by "mov[ing] down into the depths of the ground of their being" (89). What Antoinette,

Esther, Narrator, and Nora should experience to move forward in this part of the journey, Murdock explains, is the spiritual experience of "moving more deeply into self rather than out of self" (89); they need to move down into the depths to reclaim the parts of themselves that split off when they were abandoned by their mothers and when their mirrors of the feminine were shattered. Yet Esther buries everything that she should be uncovering, should be exploring: the snow is numbing and covering her landscape like the trees and grassland that sit waist-high under floodwater; like the rolling lawns of the cemetery in which she "buries" Joan, which are knee-deep in snow with tombstones rising out of it like smokeless chimneys. Rather than delving into her depths, Esther has buried everything for a temporary recovery.

Although Narrator in *Surfacing* can be seen to make some progress through Murdock's model of the heroine's journey to reconnect with the feminine, she remains trapped in the private sphere and, as Adrienne Rich argues, is "no free woman, no feminist; her way of dealing with male-identification, the struggle with a male culture, has been to numb herself, to believe she can't love" (242). She remains trapped by her father's solution.

Although Nora finally "allows" herself her anger, she is so consumed by it that she is murderous, bordering on suicidal; like Antoinette, she could burn a house down, but just by looking at the structure. In these final pages, we see embodied in Nora the French feminist belief that this type of madness, this all-consuming rage, will be the emotion that is actually freeing. Yet in the end it is not. Nora's final words, that she is angry enough "before I die to fucking well live. Just watch me," leaves an unknown space in which we ask, could she really figure out how to live in all that rage? If she could, how did she? Just like the other protagonists, we leave Nora on the edge, consumed by rage, madness, hatred, confusion too, and with all the best intentions of doing something, but then not doing anything, not answering the question, How does one move forwards now?

Murdock explains that a personal descent is a sacred journey but, in our culture, is often categorized as depression that must be medicated, shocked, and eliminated as soon as possible. Even though shock treatment may have temporarily lifted the bell jar so that Esther can breathe, as she says at the end of the novel, she is still "blank and stopped as a dead baby" in a world that is a "bad dream." Esther's "recovery" is nothing more than a temporary "forgetfulness," a "kind snow" that has numbed and covered her emotions and behaviour, but not treated them or the sources of her illness. At Joan's funeral, Esther wonders what she is burying—Esther buries her mental illness, like the image of trees and the grassland half submerged beneath water, but there is still the "black shadow": "Under the deceptively clean and level slate the topography was the same." As Antoinette remarks, "you can pretend for a long time, but one day it all falls away and you are alone." Esther moves to action too soon because the pain—both for her and her doctors—of holding the tension of the unknown is unbearable. But this means that true healing cannot occur: "If we abort our process we never allow ourselves to come full term" (Murdock, 108). Nora, too, seems so enraged and hell-bent on proving everyone wrong that she seems as though she is doing just what she did in the past, again and again—acting without actually working through her emotional and psychological process. This rage is, in fact, maddening.

Thus, in our vertical and horizontal textual analysis we can see that there are correlations with and departures from Murdock's heroine's journey, and that there are many similarities between the texts themselves. Most importantly, we discover that they all close at the point of narrative descent in the heroine's journey, with no manifestation of any ascent.

Madness as narrative closure in the heroine's journey

Caroline Rody argues that the rebellious heroine, Antoinette, furiously opposes her pre-scripted fate and is thus "our greatest figure for the resisting female figure" (302); Elaine Showalter states that Esther is "reborn at the end of the book" (218); and Barbara Hill Rigney proclaims that *Surfacing*'s protagonist has surfaced from madness and is finally secure in an undivided self (114). I would also argue that Claire Messud believed her ending to be a great victory for Nora and for all "women upstairs." Yet, reading the four novels using Murdock's heroine's journey, the protagonists can be seen to remain trapped both figuratively, by extant power structures, and literally, by a dark passage, a mental asylum, surrounding trees, and blinding rage. In the end, the protagonists remain straitjacketed by social constraints and oppressed as victims of patriarchal hegemony. Simply put, Antoinette, Esther, Narrator, and Nora are more terrified and trapped than traitorous and triumphant—they are prisoners of their descent.

Notes

1   For the purpose of this study, I will call Antoinette's husband Rochester, though he is never named in Rhys's text.

2   Obeah is a term used in the West Indies to refer to folk magic, sorcery.

4

The eternal
madwoman

"I'm still defeated by the conundrum of God.
But I have the devil clear."
"And what's he?"
"Not seeing whole."
—John Fowles (207)

There exists across novels containing literary madwomen a pattern that reflects madness as narrative closure: the journey of what I define as the "eternal madwoman." This leads us to draw a revised version of Murdock's heroine's journey, one that is adapted to the specific experiences noted in the four novels discussed in the previous chapter, and that stops halfway through its progression. In this way, what interests me, as it did Heller in her study of female adolescence in contemporary American fiction, is a recurrent pattern discernible less by content than by form (14).

The eternal madwoman model traps the protagonist in

psychological descent and demonstrates the ways in which self-reflexivity and narrative fragmentation actually affirm the status quo rather than subvert it. This structure leaves feminism no means of legitimating its own oppositional position and, in fact, digs out the ground from under its own feet. From this perspective, it is possible to indicate some of the difficulties that arise from a privileging of madness-as-rebellion as the foundation for a political aesthetic. In fact, this narrative structure traps women in the private sphere, resulting in what Felski terms the "prevailing ideologies of femininity as the sphere of otherness, of antireason, and anticulture, which continue to exercise a powerful influence" (*Beyond Feminist Aesthetics*, 150).

This is not to negate the importance of experimental and modernist feminist literature, but, rather, to argue for its disassociation from political efficacy and subversive rebellion. This model captures the protagonist in a marginal space; any advocacy of this position as positive, or even the preferred state of the "feminine," further reinforces the precise marginality of women that feminism should seek to question; Greene explains it well when she states that "as long as each woman is isolated ... [and] her anguish is so private that it cannot even be named, there is no possibility of change" (46).

The decipherable patterns of inner turmoil described in the eternal madwoman's journey reflect the lack of any outward expression of female development; fighting patriarchal standards, female protagonists thus engage in a kind of internalized self-combat. Fetishized and codified by a feminist literary system, which promotes irrationality, the female protagonist who remains faithful to this inauthentic image of female rebellion is, as Heller argues, "led ever deeper into self-denial, passivity and inertia" (12).

The eternal madwoman's journey thus cannot be understood as the liberation of a true woman's writing from the straitjacket of a patriarchal system of representation.

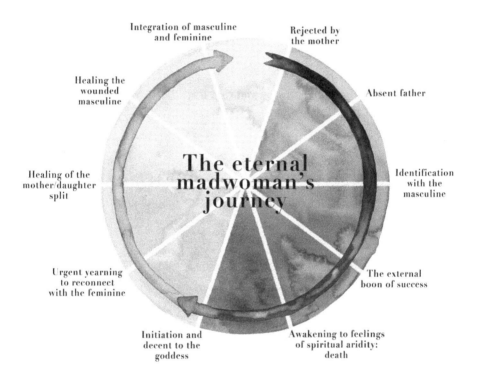

Figure 2: The eternal madwoman's journey

Just as female protagonists in nineteenth-century literature remain entrapped by social restrictions and definitions of female "goodness" that demand their passivity, submission, and obedience, so too does the eternal madwoman's journey entrap the female protagonist in social restrictions and definitions of female rebellion that demand mental instability and the inability to function in society.

Further, interpreting the eternal madwoman's journey as subversive reinscribes at the level of theoretical abstraction those gender specifications whose inevitability feminists, as Felski argues, should be calling into question. It reaffirms "existing structures and women's traditionally marginalized role" because it reinforces the "devaluation of women as active participants in the public sphere" (*Beyond Feminist Aesthetics*, 40). It extrapolates an abstract dualism grounded in the equation of the masculine with happy endings and the feminine with madness. I therefore believe an important question, as mentioned earlier, for feminist literary critics in the twenty-first century is, "Why do happy endings continue to be considered so unfeminist?"

While literary critics often celebrate women's writing during the mid- to late-twentieth century as throwing off the shackles of tradition, creating completely new stories, and telling the unvarnished truth of women's lives, I would argue that this view is actually mistaken. In fact, many of these novels simply abandon the heroine's journey halfway through and, therefore, have merely tinkered with traditional forms of narrative. In this way, writers of the eternal madwoman's journey have modified existing plots to conform to the contemporary social and ideological conditions shaping women's lives as they have been affected by feminism. Yet, while the authors have ruptured the narrative structure, it is feminist literary critics who have interpreted this rupture as feminist rebellion.

A new reading: madness as descent rather than dissent

Viewing madness as a metaphor for rebellion, as dissent against patriarchal power, has problematic implications. The eternal madwoman model reinforces Donaldson's argument that the madness/rebellion configuration subtly reinforces what has become an almost monolithic way of reading mental illness within feminist literary criticism and, perhaps, in the wider culture of women's studies. This model also demonstrates that madness itself offers women little opportunity for true resistance or productive rebellion, since the eternal madwoman never progresses beyond the descent stage of her journey.

A fictional character's narrative decline into darkness is a well-worn path. Campbell calls this trajectory the down-going, or *kathodos* (*The Hero with a Thousand Faces*, 21); Todorov defines it as a gradual "breakdown in equilibrium" (39). Interestingly, Charlotte Brontë also refers to this narrative and journey structure in the epitaph she wrote for Lucy Snowe in *Villette* (1853): "The orb of your life is not to be rounded; for you the crescent-phase must suffice."[1] In the previous analyses, we see *The Bell Jar, Wide Sargasso Sea, Surfacing,* and *The Woman Upstairs* travelling down the right-hand side of Murdock's heroine's journey, yet the characters remain trapped halfway, unable to move beyond the stage of initiation and descent to the goddess.

Yet, this pathway of descent differs from the trajectory of what Aristotle would define as "tragedy." While the down-going is defined as *kathodos*, the up-coming is defined as *anodos* and, together, they create a story process defined as *katharsis*. In Aristotle's definition of tragedy, this dual process and purging must occur; therefore, even in a tragic narrative structure there are two-crescents, a complete cycle, a descent and ascent. Rather than a tragedy, this structure of the eternal madwoman's journey is more akin to Booker's inverted narrative.

Christopher Booker explores the notion of a narrative's separated hemicycle in *The Seven Basic Plots: Why We Tell Stories* (2004). He explains that the ancient Greeks were the first to ask, "What is it that prevents a hero or heroine from transformation and brings them so inexorably to catastrophe?" (569) Their answer invoked the notion of *hubris*. Yet, Booker explains, we have misunderstood this concept. Rather than being a form of overwhelming pride and reckless arrogance, the term is actually derived from the word *hyper*, meaning "over"—an allusion to "stepping over the bounds," a defiance of the cosmic order, that state of perfect balance which ultimately, as Todorov and Campbell also believe, holds the universe together. Booker takes this notion of *hubris* and extends it beyond the genre of tragedy to explain narratives that are, by his definition, inverted. He builds on their universal narrative to suggest essential values that are programmed into our unconscious. The essential message implicit in this programming, he argues, is that the central goal of human life is to achieve the state of perfect balance that we recognize as maturity; and that the central enemy in reaching that goal is our capacity to be held back by the "deforming and ultimately self-destructive power of ego-centricity" (569).

Certainly, Booker is borrowing such notions from Freud and Jung. Yet he applies the hypothesis to storytelling over the past two centuries to argue that a fundamental shift has taken place, in many modern stories, in the psychological "centre of gravity" from which they have been told. Booker argues that modern narratives have become detached from their underlying archetypal purpose and that they have taken on a fragmented, subjective nature, becoming more like personal dreams or fantasies. In many ways, we can see this type of narrative mirroring the type of irrational chaos championed by French feminist criticism as a site for personal and political rebellion.

The eternal madwoman's narrative structure is similarly detached from its underlying archetypal journey and, therefore, focuses on the descent without the necessary ascent; unlike a tragedy, whose structure is complete, the severed narrative descent creates a frozen form. In turn, I argue against the madness-as-rebellion metaphor and for a new reading of madness in feminist literature in the twentieth century as descent rather than dissent. Rather than rebelling against patriarchal assumptions, this narrative structure merely reinforces gendered stereotypes of females being predisposed to madness.

The only rebellion, if any, that can be seen in this journey model is that of the writer cutting the narrative in half. That act can only be rebellious if one views the journey model as a patriarchal structure rather than a humanistic narrative model. Furthermore, even if one views the structure as oppressive to writers, the technique of cutting the sphere in two is actually destructive to the female protagonist.

Rupturing the descent/ascent binary

In the construction of the eternal madwoman's journey, we see a narrative representation of a crescent-shaped life—a half-life— cut short at the end of a treacherous descent. Thus, instead of experiencing the personal growth associated with this mythical structure, the women become locked in a descent into darkness. These texts, which sever the narrative from formerly conventional structures of fiction, may momentarily imagine a world devoid of the patriarchal expectation of the domestic, yet they ultimately leave their characters suffering feelings of futility, despair, and resignation. Interestingly, the way in which I use this term "half-life" in literature is reminiscent of the scientific "half-life," which usually describes the decay of discrete entities, such as radioactive atoms. In the descent, we also see an element of decay; there is a rotting away or decomposition of self endured by the protagonists.

Although previous interpretations have viewed madness as narrative closure as an act of rebellion, by contemplating the novels' narrative structures as depictions of the heroine's journey, we are able to illuminate new meanings. Rather than rallying against societal assumptions of and constraints on women, the eternal madwoman, in the descent phase of a mythic journey, has little personal or political efficacy. Therefore, through this new reading, the protagonists can be seen as more tragic than transformational.

While feminist theorists such as Baym, Caminero-Santangelo, and Donaldson have argued theoretically against the madness as resistance metaphor and, indeed, against the textual approach expounded by French feminists, I argue that this analysis supports their arguments in a more concrete way.

This new reading also poses the question, have we, in our eagerness to deconstruct what we believe to be patriarchal structures and provide alternatives to individual quests, actually prevented our female protagonists from any real character development and, in turn, power? When the literary madwoman or, as I call her here, the eternal madwoman is considered as person first and metaphor second, it is difficult to answer anything but yes. Yet, just as there is academic debate about whether madness in literature is rebellious, so too is there debate around whether a ruptured narrative sequence subverts a patriarchal structure.

Rupture as rebellion

A powerful narrative binary can be found in the opposition of descent/ascent. Put together, the two halves can be interpreted as the patriarchal plot structure criticized by many French feminist critics. Just as Cixous argues that hysteria is a force that dismantles structure, so too do we see, in this model, madness as a force that separates the mythic descent/ascent binary. Thus we see certain feminist approaches to madness as prioritizing descent as a way to subvert the supposed masculine expectation of ascent; a journey for the heroine towards either romantic love or death. Yet, it will be explained throughout the following chapters, there are other forms of ascent than patriarchal notions of love and family. While they do not argue specifically for madness as rebellion or for the literary madwoman as a revolutionary figure, there are a number of feminist literary critics (including Rachel DuPlessis, Molly Hite, Alison Booth and Caroline Rody, all discussed below, as well as Ellen Friedman and Gayle Greene) who argue for the efficacy of ruptured narratives.[2] In fact, between 1980 and 2000 there was considerable focus by feminist literary critics on the ways in which twentieth-century women writers broke from narrative convention and, indeed, the ways in which this rupture was rebellious.

If, as I argue, the ways in which critics choose to read texts is ultimately a political act, then what does our reading of the madwoman as rebel say about us in the twenty-first century? I would argue, firstly, that it points to an ever-increasing divide between institutional feminism and everyday feminism and, secondly, that it also points towards a scepticism regarding happiness. It is true that the concept of a happy ending in literature has in the past been associated with patriarchal edifices such as a nineteenth-century definition of marriage. Yet, feminism has fought for growth in all our relationships, in the workplace and within ourselves, over the past eighty years and, although there is still so much work to be done, surely we have come far enough to understand that happiness can come in different guises? By taking issue with the current trend in feminist literary criticism, which fetishizes irrationality, this book argues for optimism. Since, as Felski argues, narratives constitute "one of the most important ways in which ideologies are concretized in relation to life experience," the encouragement and consequent reading of new plots for women that emphasize self-actualization rather than self-harm needs to be "welcomed as an indication of the influence of feminism upon the cultural and ideological domain" (*Beyond Feminist Aesthetics*, 152). This is not to deny the validity of criticism influenced by French feminism but, rather, to call into question the argument that a preference for antireason, antistructure, indeed antihappiness, is the only valid approach to reading feminist literature; and, in turn, to call into question dichotomies that have been recognized as sterile for over thirty years but that still persist.

It is interesting to note that this surge of feminist literary criticism beginning in 1980 mirrors, and in fact takes up the baton from, the previously discussed critics writing between 1960 and 1980 who supported the madness-as-rebellion trope. Within both groups, we see not only a focus on rebelling against patriarchal expectations (in behaviour and narrative structure respectively) but on the writer's technique as the rebellious act. While many French feminists supported an upheaval of sentence structure and a newly defined female writing, the feminist literary critics discussed below argue for the subversive effect of a writer's structural choices.

Rachel DuPlessis, in her text *Writing Beyond the Ending* (1985), would call the crescent-shaped life represented in the eternal madwoman's journey a "ruptured narrative": an invented strategy that severs the narrative from formerly conventional structures of fiction. Overall, DuPlessis's hypothesis is that the only resolution available to writers of the nineteenth century was marriage or death, and that this fate of female characters expressed attitudes toward family, sexuality, and gender. She identifies a number of narrative strategies invented or deployed by female writers of the twentieth century explicitly to delegitimize romance plots and related narratives. One of the primary approaches is what DuPlessis calls "breaking the sequence"; that is, to question the construction of gender in narrative form, a writer must distance the reader from "codes of the expected narrative and from patterns of response that had seemed to command universal or natural status" (20). DuPlessis argues that the only way authors can reinterpret the lives of the women they depict is to write outside the terms of the novel's script, a strategy that forces the author to invent a narrative that offers an alternative to individual quests.

While DuPlessis's seminal study of twentieth-century literature provides insightful, original, and nuanced revelations, she, too, promotes the "rejection of dominant narratives" and displacement, erosion, or removal of expected paradigms as successful feminist dissent (20–21). Her overall focus is on the approach to narrative as feminist revolt, the writer's revolt, the story structure rather than the story content.

Similarly, Molly Hite, in *The Other Side of the Story*, also provides a study of the radical innovations in narrative form attempted by a number of influential contemporary women fiction writers— notably Jean Rhys, Doris Lessing, Alice Walker, and Margaret Atwood. Like DuPlessis, Hite argues that narratological rupture is rebellious. In fact, she goes as far as to say women's narrative innovations are more radical in their implications than the dominant modes of fictional experiment, and more radical precisely because the context for innovation is a critique of a culture and a literary tradition apprehended as profoundly masculinist.

Hite also believes there are two approaches to feminist narratology: firstly, the American feminist criticism, which concentrates on the women who write and the female experience represented, presuming a realist or even "confessional mode" and, secondly, those aligned with French feminist criticism, which concentrates on the decentring and destabilizing tendencies of twentieth-century experimental writing (16). Thus, Hite would align many of the feminist critics included in this section, such as DuPlessis, with French feminist criticism—which argues that experiments with structure often result in effective subversion—and thus also with the critics who argue for the madness-as-rebellion metaphor.

Similarly, writing technique, as opposed to female experience, is emphasized in *Famous Last Words: Changes in Gender and Narrative Closure* (1993), in which editor Alison Booth argues that there is a renewed impetus for talking about heroines in feminist literary criticism and that no point in the protagonist's narrative bears more conventional weight than her ending. She also argues that endings have seldom been anything more than double or binary choices for most female characters: marriage or death. By choosing an ending other than the binary, Booth argues, and thus changing the expected trajectory of their protagonists, writers attempt to achieve canon reformation, to advocate alternative knowledge paradigms, and to decentralize sources of authority. Booth asks the questions, "Has the implementation of modernist and experimentalist fiction assisted in the escape of the female subject?" and "Has the breakdown of closed traditional narrative released the female subject?" (9). Yet, although these questions are pertinent to feminist literary criticism, the collection covers so many contexts and also so many types of texts, that Booth is unable to contribute any answers to these questions—other than that fixed answers are counterproductive.

Booth's introduction is insightful but conveys such a reluctance to make generalizations that her statements contradict each other: she argues that there are important patterns everywhere in narrative, but that emphasizing these patterns can prescribe essentialist analysis; she argues that formal experimentation corresponds with more open gender relations in narrative, but that realistic conventions can provide a steadier vehicle for feminist argument than experiments in nonlinear technique; she argues that open form is a useful tool for feminist writers but also that they can reinstate closed form to powerful effect; and, finally, she states that form and ideology collaborate, but that saying so too neatly points to a careless examination of a text.

Certainly, it is difficult to criticize Booth for anything in her introduction, since she covers all bases and, on a number of occasions, warns against tempting generalizations. Overall, however, these contradictions cause confusion, and there appears to be no clear point to Booth's introduction other than to introduce the collection's writers. The only argument to which Booth yields is that there are many ways novelists have devised to arrive at the actual last word. I have included Booth's introduction because, if one reads between the lines, she does seem to have a preference for disrupting narratives in feminist writing, and because she has chosen and edited the chapters within the collection. I also wanted to include a brief discussion of this introduction because it is a fitting example of why feminist literary criticism is as much in a state of paralysis as the eternal madwoman. As discussed in the introduction, feminist literary critics are often so reluctant to make any brave or bold arguments for fear of dismissal that their writing fails to contribute any original outcomes. Instead, too much of their writing displays circular logic that covers all angles and contexts, until we are all confused as to why the feminist critic is writing at all.

Within Booth's book, however, Caroline Rody's chapter on *Wide Sargasso Sea* argues specifically for narrative disruption as feminist rebellion. And, indeed, Booth's focus on this chapter in her introduction suggests a propensity for similar beliefs. Yet, even though Rody does mention the character's situation and experience as subversive, she focuses, like Booth, on the writer's technique, arguing that although the text does not save Antoinette from her plot's downward trajectory to madness and death, the "novel's trajectory is upward, toward liberation." Rody, in fact, argues that Rhys's ending in *Wide Sargasso Sea* is "triumphant" and "revisionist" and that this literary madwoman is "our greatest figure for the resisting female" (302).

Yet, Rody at times suffers from the same contradictory ailment as Booth does in her introduction, as when she states (aligning her arguments with Friedman) that the very fact that Antoinette is restricted to a predetermined narrative is liberating (312). In fact, Rody herself states that, in effect, Bertha/Antoinette in *Jane Eyre* and *Wide Sargasso Sea* both burn down houses (or demonstrate the will to) and that, therefore, "only the novel survives to stand in the clear space of freedom" (312). Even though Booth explains in her introduction that the writers have been encouraged to look at their protagonists as real people in the real world, Rody cannot truly argue that Rhys's ending liberates Bertha from the attic; she can only argue that the text itself rebels against "oppressive political structures and literary plots" (313).

It is difficult to understand how Rody can argue for *Wide Sargasso Sea* as a tribute to potential readers when the ending of the novel can imagine no alternative to entrapment in the moment before a suicidal act. Yet, while I disagree with Rody's arguments, rather than dismissing them I aim to embrace them as contributing knowledge about the literary madwoman to feminist literary criticism and providing an analysis to build upon, and against. It must be said, however, that if Rhys gives us a paradigm for a revisionary twentieth-century art that draws power from a century in women's lives to light a common future passage, it is a passage I would be very reluctant to travel. Although the severed narrative revises the heroes' quest narrative, there is no freedom, no emancipation, no resolution in this revision.

This entrapment can be seen in our reading of the four novels using the model of the heroine's journey. In the end of *The Bell Jar*, *Wide Sargasso Sea*, *Surfacing*, and *The Woman Upstairs*, the women are stuck in their journey, unable to move beyond their descent into darkness. They are on thresholds, trapped in a kind of limbo or purgatory. We leave Antoinette roaming the hallways of

Thornfield thinking about burning down the house; Esther in a room in the mental asylum, not knowing if she has been determined "well" enough to be released; Narrator standing behind and in between trees as Joe calls her name and she remains uncertain whether to respond; and Nora consumed by her maddening rage with only the promise that she will show people how she will live. The four women are on the brink of action, yet nothing has happened to move them past meeting their shadow self. There does not seem to be, as Caminero-Santangelo argues, any form of effective rebellion in this paralysis.

While Booth, DuPlessis, and Booker discuss ruptures in expected narrative structures, many writers in the twentieth century have, in fact, specifically cut the quest narrative in half. Yet, as Makward asserts, this deconstruction is highly problematic, since the theory of rupture is dangerously close to repeating in deconstructive language the traditional assumptions (96). While texts that end in madness may momentarily envision a world devoid of patriarchal oppression, these writers are finally unable to create that world and, in the end, their characters succumb to feelings of futility, despair, and resignation. Just as madness-as-rebellion can actually function as if in collusion with the cultural conditions that produced it, so too can the narrative structure—this ruptured quest—ultimately trap the woman in eternal silence. Arguably, when one considers the female experience as paramount, the ruptured narrative structure used to promote madness as closure is an unsuccessful feminist writing device.

Thus, there are two primary reasons a ruptured narrative does not act as successful feminist rebellion. Firstly, I—like other feminist critics such as Felksi and Moi—do not believe that women's writing that challenges form is feminist simply because it is experimental; secondly, and most importantly for this book, even if the act of rupturing a narrative could be seen as feminist if it results in an eternal madwoman, it is an unsuccessful feminist device. It is difficult to understand how a structural approach, which creates an eternal madwoman, which in fact traps her in the darkness of descent, in a powerless stature, can be seen as an effective feminist writing approach. Yet critics such as Booth, Hite, Rody, DuPlessis, and Ellen Friedman do so by separating the writing technique from the female experience. I would argue that this separation mirrors the separation of the madwoman as metaphor from notions of mental illness. In both instances, a theoretical approach transcends female experience. This division is often represented as that between American feminism and French feminism—one expressive and typically content-based, the other linguistically conscious and antihumanist. As explained in the introduction, I argue—aligning myself with current critical disability studies approaches to literature—for a focus on the literary madwoman as individual first before metaphorical interpretation. Yet this focus is also often represented in American feminism, which privileges the characters' experience over the writers' language.

It should be noted that I believe that writers such as Jean Rhys, Sylvia Plath, Margaret Atwood and Claire Messud (amongst others) are innovative narrative strategists. But there is a difference between experimentation and emancipation. Essentially, critics who support the rupture of narrative sequences as effective feminist rebellion, as everything from to triumphant to liberating, focus on the writer's technique. Interestingly and, I believe, importantly, none of these writers would have called themselves "feminist"; in fact they often fought against the label.

Overall, I take issue with the current strand of feminist literary theory that argues that structure in fiction is a masculine device; that plot linearity implies a story's purposeful forward movement and the movement to closure are necessarily part of a dominant fictional structure that is metonymic, reflecting cultural values in its order and progression and therefore represents patriarchal mastery in Western culture. I argue, along with theorists such as Rita Felski, that this common perception in feminist theory is highly flawed. Yet I go further than Felski and argue that, by perpetuating this single belief and by basing much of feminist literary theory on its premise, this approach to feminist literary criticism further reinforces females' historical lack of personal power, and social and political influence. This is because, as Kristeva argued, a feminist language that refuses to participate in supposed "masculine" discourse, that places its future entirely in a feminine, semiotic discourse, risks being relegated to the outskirts of what is considered socially and politically significant. Like the eternal madwoman, feminist literary criticism, by defining fictional structures as "masculine" and focusing on the irrational and experimental as "feminine," has excluded women's writing and theory from the significance they deserve. By reading feminist texts through a structure such as the heroine's journey, a monomyth is humanist rather than feminine or masculine, I believe we are able to redirect feminist literary theory into public discourse.

The deconstructionist celebration of the eternal madwoman as a privileged form of subversion has been led astray by the belief that narrative structure is intrinsically masculine. It is unquestionably important and necessary for oppressed social groups to draw attention to the rigidity of dominant discourses that exclude or marginalize them; but, as Felski argues, the "attempt to argue for the possibility of a domain outside the constraints of symbolic signification necessarily results in self-defeating self-contradiction" (*Beyond Feminist Aesthetics*, 61).

Not only is the celebration of the eternal madwoman as feminist rebel by literary critics problematic, it relies upon dangerous beliefs and assumptions; namely, that the reason this writing technique is subversive is because it cuts the monomyth structure in half. This approach equates all existing and historical discursive structures with masculine repression, failing to realize that, for feminism to have political efficacy, it must celebrate and call for literary female protagonists who influence the public sphere. The literary madwoman, though, has been cut off from the public sphere, doomed to reside in the nether regions of personal darkness. As Felski argues, the denial of the public sphere is a failure of feminist literary criticism because a feminist critique of patriarchal values cannot occur outside ideological and social structures in some privileged space.

Felski, in fact, argues that there exists "no necessary relationship between feminism and experimental form, and that a text can thus be defined as feminist only insofar as its content or the context of its reception promote such a reading" (*Beyond Feminist Aesthetics*, 59). An exploration of avant-garde form can constitute an important part of an oppositional women's culture, but

> *the fragmentation and subversion of patterns of meaning do not in themselves bear any relationship to a feminist position and will be perceived to do so only if the themes explored in the text bear some relation to feminist concerns—if, for example, the text seeks to undermine an obviously patriarchal ideological position.*
> (Beyond Feminist Aesthetics, 32)

The ruptured narrative model outlined in this chapter, where writers have cut the monomyth model short, could be argued to be a feminist act as it escapes the nineteenth century dichotomy of death or marriage. Yet the model used in this textual analysis, the heroine's journey model, does not include death or marriage as an option for narrative closure. Thus, to interpret the ruptured narrative of the eternal madwoman's journey as rebellious, a feminist critic would have to assume that any monomyth model, no matter what the prescribed ending, is patriarchal and repressive simply because it is linear and structural, and that any rupture of it is feminine, and therefore feminist, simply because it opens and breaks that structure. That is to say, they would have to argue that narrative as goal-orientated form is in some way quintessentially masculine and limits meaning by operating a linear and instrumental syntax. Felski argues that this view is "not only politically counterproductive for feminism" but "inappropriately abstract" (*Beyond Feminist Aesthetics*, 32). I agree but take this notion a step further and argue that this approach by feminist literary critics is not just undesirable; in idealizing madness as rebellion it is actually harmful to feminism's quite specific and determinate social goals.

Narrative structure as human rather than masculine

In 1989, Gillian Beer asked the important question, "Can the female self be expressed through plot or must it be conceived in resistance to plot?" (117). I argue in this book, and this section in particular, that not only should the female self be expressed through plot, but that the fact that she has been prevented from doing so goes against all research into the evolutionary, biological, and cognitive purposes of structured storytelling. Thus, I am interested in the political and psychological dimensions of literary forms and aim to question at the most fundamental level linguistic and textual structure.

Current feminist literary criticism is defined by an increasing preoccupation with theory, as critics increasingly move toward linguistically based methods of analysis such as semiotics and deconstruction. Therefore, the political function of literature as art has been redefined: it is not the "text which reflects female experience that best serves feminist interests, but rather the work which disrupts the very structures of symbolic discourse" (Felski, Beyond Feminist Aesthetics, 30). For this argument to stand, as previously argued, one must assume that narrative structure is oppressive, negative, a tyrannical tool of patriarchal hegemony; that any rupture of this structure undermines the linguistic conventions of a phallocentric symbolic order.

Literature's social function is vital to an emancipatory feminist politics; yet narratives cannot serve this role if experimental writing constitutes the only truly subversive practice and more conventional forms, such as realism, are considered inferior. Furthermore, poststructuralism, where it denies the subject altogether, jettisons, as Felski argues, "the chance of challenging the *ideology of the subject* (as male, white, and middle class) by developing alternative and different notions of subjectivity" (*Beyond Feminist Aesthetics*, 44; emphasis in original). If we define narrative structure as just as much a part of the female psyche as of the male, then the rupture of this narrative cannot, in and of itself, be seen as rebellious. It is important to note that my arguments do not aim to question the importance of revisionist and experimental writers, nor to undermine the impact of academic work that brings the tradition of women's experimental fiction into view, such as that of Friedman and Fuchs. Rather, what I argue is that the assumption that narrative structure is a product of a purely patriarchal Western culture is not only inherently flawed, but simply incorrect; and that the arguments that have been based upon this presumption have been detrimental not only to feminist literary analysis but to our approach to storytelling.

Although an extensive exploration of the origin of storytelling, and the ways in which our brains and culture crave structured storytelling, is beyond the scope of this book, I believe it is important to touch on this area of research. By telling stories, we make sense of the world, whether we are male or female, young or old; we order its events and find meaning in them by assimilating them to more or less familiar narratives. It is this human ability to organize experience into narrative form that we call "narrative intelligence." Certainly, there has been much work done in academia around the fact that we are storytelling animals; around the argument that we, as humans, have survived and thrived due to our ability and compulsion to tell stories. A focus on the importance of storytelling characterizes many academic fields, including computing, law, medicine, psychology, business and branding, sociology, aged care, ethics, biology, literary studies; I would go as far as to say there are few areas of research in which storytelling has not figured as an important phenomenon. Yet, interestingly, research into structured story-telling, into why we tell stories (whether verbally or in written form), has rarely been integrated into feminist—especially literary feminist—studies. I would hypothesize that this is because research into this area might undermine much of the French feminist criticism approach to literature.

Although the Jonathan Gottschall's highly digestible *The Storytelling Animal* took academic arguments to the masses, and makes important points about the necessity of storytelling for the survival of the human species, I would argue that the research of distinguished scholar Brian Boyd in *On the Origins of Stories: Evolution, Cognition and Fiction* (2009) offers a more rigorous and relevant study. Boyd argues that our minds are shaped to understand structure; brains evolved, he explains, not to give humans rich inner lives—though we are delighted they do—but to permit creatures that have them to make better decisions (162). Feminist literary studies' focus on irrational and chaotic semiotics, and narrative rupture in fiction, has precluded feminist literature playing a role as educator, as a map on how to live a better life, how to make better decisions.

The difficulty of programming computers to understand natural-language narratives has, as Boyd argues, "made plain how richly our minds process the world so that we can understand events and stories from the sparest information" (189). In turn, we could respond to French feminist criticism's argument that narrative structure is masculine by counterarguing that this must mean that men's brains work differently from women's. In fact, much of our ability and inclination to understand, recall, represent, and invent events precedes language; our structured storytelling instinct thus has biocultural origins. Simply put, storytelling develops spontaneously and without training in childhood in the form of pretend play and, even as adults, we can and want to tell, read, and listen to fiction. In fact, Boyd also argues that structured fictional storytelling is more about play than survival. These stories must have a certain structure for our brains to respond to them: "a large-scale structure, with distinct and well-formed episodes, especially in terms of characters' goals" (186). I would ask the question, if we assume that structured storytelling is masculine in origin, does this mean that only men play? That women do not?

It is impossible to speak of masculine and feminine narrative structure in any meaningful sense, since storytelling and the structures it requires are humanistic. Narrative is always strategic, for both teller and listener, and it is not the structure of narrative that is inherently masculine or oppressive, but its content.

Notes

1   Rebecca Fraser applies this quote to Charlotte Brontë's life in her biography *Charlotte Brontë* (London: Vintage, 1988), 483.

2   It should be noted that Marianna Torgovnick wrote Closure in the Novel around this time in 1981. While she focuses on endings in fiction she does not extrapolate this into commentary on narrative closure as a feminist tool.

5

Resolving the eternal madwoman

Midway upon the journey of our life
I found myself within a forest dark,
For the straightforward pathway had been lost ...
So bitter is it, death is little more.

—Dante Alighieri (ll. 1–7)

R eading the madwoman's narrative against the model of the heroine's journey reveals an abrupt closure. While in the previous chapter I focused on the eternal madwoman's narratological right hemicycle, and how her resultant madness can be seen as a descent rather than dissent, in this chapter I aim to answer, from both a psychological (character's psyche) and narratological (external to character) perspective, the question of what keeps the madwoman trapped halfway through the heroine's journey. This can be seen as the coming together of the generalized American feminist theory of female experience and French feminist theory of textual analysis.

Just as I aim to redefine approaches such as narratology, structuralism, and myth as humanistic rather than masculine, and in turn to reunite their approaches with feminism, so too I aim to reconfigure psychoanalysis's relationship with feminist literary criticism. In this way, I aim to further the work of Rigney, who argues that although a psychoanalytic approach to feminist literary criticism has been considered by French feminist criticism to be both a product and a defence of the status quo—a patriarchal society—feminism and psychology should be reconciled in the area of literary criticism (3).

The eternal madwoman's encounter with darkness

The relationship between the mythic journey and Jungian psychology in many ways began when Joseph Campbell recognized Jung's fundamental psychological structures and stages within numerous myths from disparate times and regions. From this realization, Campbell created a standardized language that made it possible to uncover and communicate the underlying archetypal structure of these narrative traditions. One of Campbell's most overt uses of Jungian psychology is the concept of "meeting the shadow," which he describes as finding oneself "in the belly of the whale." Campbell found that the image of the dark womb is a recurrent theme in storytelling. "The Eskimo of Bering Strait" tells of the trickster-hero, Raven, who darts into the belly of the whale; "The Zulus" tells a story of two children and their mother who are swallowed by an elephant; the Irish hero Finn Mac Cumhaill was swallowed by a monster; the little German girl Red Ridinghood was swallowed by a wolf; Polynesian hero Maui was swallowed by his great-great-grandmother; and the whole Greek pantheon, with the sole exception of Zeus, was swallowed by its father, Kronos (The Hero with a Thousand Faces, 249). This popular motif gives emphasis to the lesson that the passage of the threshold is a form of self-annihilation.

Variations of Campbell's journey also reference the belly of the whale or dark passage. Frankel defines it as a "descent into darkness," Hudson calls it the "crisis," and Vogler calls it the "inmost cave":

> *The way grows narrow and dark. You must go alone on hands and knees as you feel the earth press close around you. You can hardly breathe. Suddenly you come out into the deepest chamber and find yourself face-to-face with a towering figure, a menacing Shadow composed of all your doubts and fears.... Here, in this moment, is the chance to win all or die. No matter what you came for, it's Death that now stares back at you. Whatever the outcome of the battle, you are about to taste death and it will change you.* (143)

As early as 1912, Jung used the term "shadow side to the psyche" to characterize "unrecognized desires" and "repressed portions of the personality." In 1917, in his essay "On the Psychology of the Unconscious," Jung speaks of the personal shadow as the "other" in us: the unconscious personality of the same sex, the reprehensible inferior, the other that embarrasses or shames us. "By shadow," Jung explains, "I mean the 'negative' side of the personality, the sum of all those unpleasant qualities we like to hide, together with the insufficiently developed functions and the content of the personal unconscious" (86). It is important to note, though, that Jung did not mean "negative" in the purely moral sense. Jungian analyst Marie-Louise von Franz tells of an occasion when Jung, impatient with fellow psychologists, dismissed a nit-picking conversation about whether the shadow is illicit: "This is all nonsense. The shadow is simply the whole unconscious." Jung often wanted to clarify that the shadow is not evil. "The shadow," he explained, "is merely somewhat inferior, primitive, unadapted, and awkward; not wholly bad" (90). He battled against contradictory understandings of the shadow, and still the definitions are numerous. For the purposes of this book,

I use a definition developed from Jung and outlined by von Franz: "in the first stage of the approach to the unconscious, the shadow is simply a mythological name for all that is within me of which I cannot directly know" (2).

To the ego, the shadow may appear at first as frightening or evil, since it represents what the ego has repressed. But, with its acceptance, the shadow reveals itself as the helpful friend, helping bring to consciousness those elements of the unconscious, especially *eros*, necessary to the wholeness and health of the self. Yet, unassimilated, the shadow figure becomes evil, a constellation of all that is demonic in the dark side of the psyche, which, in itself, is ethically neutral.

In a narrative sense, then, the meeting with the shadow is crucial to the development of the self and, therefore, of a character. The shadow is the guardian of the threshold who can lead the way to selfhood. Jung himself writes that:

> *our life is like the course of the sun. In the morning it gains continually in strength until it reaches the zenith-heat of high noon. Then comes the enantiodromia: the steady forward movement no longer denotes an increase, but a decrease, in strength.... The transition from morning to afternoon means a revaluation of earlier values. There comes the urgent need to appreciate the value of the opposite of our former ideals, to perceive the error of our former truth, and to feel how much antagonism and even hatred lay in what, until now, had passed for love. (74–5)*

Here, Jung seems to describe a form of descent much like the heroine's journey and similar to that of the four female protagonists explored in the previous chapter. As Campbell notes, entering into a dark sphere on the journey to rebirth is a common image in writing. In reading *The Bell Jar, Wide Sargasso Sea, Surfacing,* and *The Woman Upstairs* through the heroine's journey, we see the protagonists entering into this darkened stage. Yet there seem to be two main differences between the shadow stories Campbell identifies and that of the madwoman. Firstly, rather than being "swallowed" by something, the women are trapped within walls—an attic, an asylum, tall trees, the Shahids' suitcase. Secondly, whereas Campbell's examples emerge from their confinement, the eternal madwoman remains in darkness: immobile at the threshold, poised to move forward but stationary, trapped within what seems like an unending pause.

Identifying the eternal madwoman's shadow

In *A Little Book on the Human Shadow*, Robert Bly describes Jung's shadow as the "long bag we drag behind us" (17). When we are one or two years old, Bly explains, we are a complete person. But one day we notice that our parents do not like certain parts of that person, saying things like, "Can't you sit still," "Don't be a cry baby," or "Don't talk back at me." Behind us, Bly believes, we have an invisible bag and, to keep our parents' love, we hide the parts of us our parents do not like. By the time we go to school our bag is quite large, and then our teachers and our friends encourage us to add to it. Bly argues that we spend our first twenty or so years stuffing the bag, and the rest of our lives trying to go through it. It is the contents of this bag that are our shadow.

The eternal madwoman has also spent her life stuffing the bag, and this load burdens Antoinette, Esther, Narrator, and Nora. In the previous chapter, we saw how the protagonists' mothers and male partners spurn specific parts of their personalities: specifically, the "feminine." It appears that four main personality traits are deemed unacceptable to the people the women love and are therefore put in each woman's "bag": creativity (Antoinette's love of nature, Esther's writing, Narrator's drawing, and Nora's miniature worlds); sensitivity (all four characters' mothers discourage an awareness of one's feelings); sensuality (Rochester, Buddy, Narrator's ex, and Mr and Mrs Shahid, all use sex as a form of manipulation and each woman is punished for desiring sex); and the maternal (Antoinette wishes to look after Rochester yet he rejects her, Esther cannot choose between motherhood and her career, Narrator is haunted by an abortion, and Nora is so consumed with her desire to be a mother that she wants to steal someone else's child). These four character traits are, as Murdock points out, often associated with femininity and with what Jung calls the anima. While the protagonists are rejected by the feminine (represented by their mothers) at the outset of their journeys, they also repress the feminine (or anima) as a consequence of these traits being deemed unacceptable by the other characters in their lives, and also, I would argue, by a patriarchal society.

This initial rejection and repression causes further disconnection from the feminine. Deena Metzger suggests that another way to understand a character's shadow is to ask the question, who or what does the character hate in an irrational way? (301) We see the three protagonists expressing aversion for the feminine. Antoinette dislikes orchids; Esther separates herself from the women in her hotel; Narrator criticizes women for being vain, whining, or submissive; Nora criticizes mothers and wives.

Therefore, in the four texts, we see the protagonists rejecting the anima due to society's, and their loved ones', disapproval of "feminine" attributes, which then causes the women to dislike those traits in other people. With this understanding, we can look at the development of madness in the four novels with new insight. I suggest that it is at the point at which the four women are forced to look into their "bags" that they descend into darkness. Antoinette battles with her repressed sexuality; Esther, rejected from the writing course, is forced to face the possibility of motherhood; Narrator must accept her role in the abortion of her unborn child and is about to again face motherhood; and Nora's repressed sexual desires are made public.

The eternal madwoman and projection

Whereas each protagonist's repression of the anima is considered her shadow, each protagonist's hatred of the "masculine" or animus is defined as her projection. Although an individual's shadow is the same sex as them, an individual's projection is a contrasexual figure. Here, we meet the anima of a man or, in the eternal madwoman's case, the animus of a woman; corresponding archetypes whose autonomy and unconsciousness explain the stubbornness of their projections. Typically, Jung *personifies* these images: the most macho of men will be harbouring a shy little girl inside him; the gentle woman may be "cohabiting psychologically with the figure of a violent hoodlum" (45).

Thus, if we apply Metzger's question to the four novels, we discover that hiding within Antoinette is a patriarchal white man; within Esther, an arrogant white doctor; within Narrator, a loud and ignorant American man; and within Nora, a father who controls the finances. Virginia Woolf, writing around the time that Jung was developing his concept of the anima, also sensed that many memorable female characters in literature were not wholly convincing as portraits of actual women. She hypothesized that male authors were portraying images of their own inner compensatory idea of femininity, in both its negative and positive dimensions, under the guise of creating fictional characters:

> It is becoming daily more evident that Lady Macbeth, Cordelia, Ophelia, Clarissa, Dora, Diana, Helen and the rest are by no means what they present to be. Some are plainly men in disguise; others represent what men would like to be, or are conscious of not being. To cast out and incorporate a person of the opposite sex all that we miss in ourselves and desire in the universe and detest in

humanity is a deep and universal instinct on the part of both men and women. Rochester is as great a travesty of the truth about men as Cordelia [the saintly self-sacrificing daughter in King Lear] is of the truth about women. (42)

In distinguishing between the truth about the sexes and the "travesty of the truth" one finds in gender stereotypes, whether in the positive terms of idealizing images or in the negative terms of scapegoating, Woolf expresses in ordinary language what Jung, as a psychologist, expresses in his descriptions of the anima and animus—although one might question whether all fictional representations of the anima and animus are untruthful, since it could be the truth of the portrayal of these characters that accounts for their popularity.

Yet there is a difference between a developed and an undeveloped animus in a woman. In the case of the eternal madwoman, she could be said to have an undeveloped animus since, as we determined previously, there is an absence of any positive, influential father figure. Interestingly, M. Esther Harding, one of Jung's earliest students, argued that the undeveloped animus is likely to appear as a group (121). Therefore, if we look at the groups the eternal madwoman characters illogically hate we can determine their projections. Antoinette detests the British patriarchy; Esther hates 1950s American culture; Narrator hates Americans; and Nora despises her society, which only wants a "good girl" a "nice girl," a "straight-A, straight-laced, good daughter."

As a postcolonial work, *Wide Sargasso Sea* indicts England's exploitative colonial empire and aligns its sympathies with the plight of the black people of the Caribbean. However, the ex-slaves despise Antoinette and her family because they are white Creoles. Although the Emancipation Act has freed the slaves by the time of Antoinette's childhood, compensation has not been granted to the island's black population, breeding hostility and resentment between servants and their white employers. The text opens with Antoinette's alienation from both black Jamaicans and white slave owners. As the text progresses, we understand Antoinette's fear of the black Jamaicans, but we also witness her hatred of the British patriarchy.

Esther's sense of alienation from the world around her springs from the expectations of her as a young woman living in 1950s America. Esther's main hatred is directed at this culture and the people who represent it, such as Buddy and Buddy's mother. She feels pulled between her desire to write and the pressure she feels to settle down and start a family. While Esther's intellectual talents earn her prizes, scholarships, and respect, many people assume that she most wants to become a wife and mother. The girls at her college mock her studiousness and only show her respect when she begins dating a handsome and well-liked boy. Her relationship with Buddy earns her mother's approval, and everyone expects Esther to marry him. Buddy assumes that Esther will drop her poetic ambitions as soon as she becomes a mother, and Esther also assumes that she cannot be both mother and poet.

Atwood packs *Surfacing* with images of Americans invading and ruining Canada. The Americans install missile silos, pepper the village with tourist cabins, leave trash everywhere, and kill for sport. Atwood depicts American expansion as a process of psychological and cultural infiltration. Narrator calls Americans a "brain disease," linking American identity to behaviours rather than nationality. To Narrator, an American is anyone who commits senseless violence, loves technology, or over-consumes. Atwood depicts American expansion as destructive and a corruptive psychological influence.

The Woman Upstairs opens and closes with Nora's almost uncontrollable anger—anger at a society that does not want one to be angry, a society that only wants a good girl, a society that, she believes, has forced her to forgo all her own desires and become "the woman upstairs."

In these four novels, the protagonists maintain their hatred towards figures of patriarchal oppression. None of the characters entertain the possibility that the attributes they hate in others may be part of themselves, since what we are unconscious of in ourselves is likely to be projected onto others. The characters can be said to remain unconscious not only of their projections, but also of the fact that their projections could tell them something about themselves.

The effect of shadow and projection omission

Denial of one's shadow and projections prevents the process of individuation. This, as can be seen in Figure 1 and the subsequent journey figures, is the main objective of the second part of the heroine's journey, the ascent. Jung explains that the consequence of this ignorance is falling victim to the shadow and, as a result, feeling constantly overwhelmed by confusion and paralysed by indecision (497). The impact of such embroilment with the shadow produces what Jung describes as "a standstill that hampers moral decisions and makes convictions ineffective ... tenebrositas, chaos, melancholia" (497). Consequently, our heroines are unable to emerge from the dark.

In the texts, we see Antoinette in the attic, bemused as to how she got there; Esther envisioning her prospects as rotten figs left to fall from a tree; Narrator indecisive about whether to walk forward towards the search party; and Nora consumed by her rage towards the outside world. Furthermore, as slaves to their shadows, the four protagonists are unable to understand that their shadows and projections are, in fact, repressed parts of themselves. Without this awareness, moving past their journey's descent and towards their ascent is impossible.

Jung, towards the end of his life, warned people trapped at

this stage of their journey: "One cannot avoid the shadow unless one remains neurotic, and as long as one is neurotic one has omitted the shadow" (545). In Jung's words, we see described the eternal madwoman, trapped in darkness, in descent, in neurosis. This state of personal and narrative ambiguity is evocative of the cultural phenomenon of the liminal space.

The eternal madwoman's attic as liminal space

Arnold Van Gennep defined the term "liminality" in his 1909 *Rites de Passage*. The most prominent types of *rites de passage* tend to accompany critical moments of transition, which all societies ritualize and publicly mark with suitable observances to acknowledge the significance of the individual; these are important times such as birth, puberty, marriage, pregnancy, and death. Van Gennep argued that all rites of transition are marked by three phases: separation, margin (or *limen*), and aggregation. This transition can be seen to display a similar trajectory to that of the heroine's journey, in which there is a separation from the feminine, a margin (threshold) at the base of the descent and then an aggregation or, as Murdock calls it, integration.

Figure 3: The heroine's journey and rites of passage

The first phase of separation comprises symbolic behaviour and signifies detachment of the individual, either from an earlier fixed point in the social structure or from a set of cultural conditions (a state). During the intervening liminal period, the state of the ritual subject (the passenger) is ambiguous; she passes through a realm that has few or none of the attributes of either the past or the coming state. In the third phase, the passage is consummated, and the subject is in a stable state once more. In anthropology, liminality is the quality of ambiguity or disorientation that occurs in the middle stage of rituals, when participants no longer hold their preritual status but have not yet begun the transition to the status they will hold when the ritual is complete.

It is this marginal stage that is of particular importance to this chapter. Also pertinent is the idea of *rites de passage*. Though not specifically outlined as such in her work, Murdock's model—and the model constructed thus far as the eternal madwoman's journey—certainly represent individuals moving through rites of passage, including changes in careers or lack thereof, motherhood or lack thereof, and movement from girlhood into young womanhood and from young womanhood into middle-age. During a ritual's liminal stage, participants stand at the threshold between their previous way of structuring their identity and a new way of life. Each of the characters in the four novels structures their identity around their external boon of success: Antoinette and her marriage, Esther and her writing career, Narrator and her pregnancy, Nora and her life with the Shahids.

The eternal madwoman as liminal persona

In 1967, in an essay titled "Betwixt and Between: The Liminal Period in Rites of Passage," Victor Turner introduced the term "liminal personae" (threshold people): those who live in an ambiguous world where one's sense of identity dissolves, to some extent, and brings about disorientation (53). These individuals are trapped in a stage of darkness, unable to move forward in their personal journey. Turner argues that we should view this period of margin or liminality as an "interstructural situation" (50). In such situations, the very structure of someone's life is temporarily suspended.

The twentieth and twenty-first century madwoman's text aimed, and still aims, to dismantle structure and, in fact, cuts an established structure into two halves. Within this description, we hear echoes of *l'écriture féminine*'s battle against binaries and their support for the chaos that unravels structure. Thus, we see the four protagonists, and subsequently our eternal madwoman character, as not only denying their shadows and projections, but also as being trapped in a period of margin during an important rite of passage. I suggest, therefore, that the eternal madwoman can be defined as a liminal persona. This individual, Turner explains, is the "structurally indefinable": she is at once no longer classified and not yet classified (49). Turner's description of the liminal persona's condition as "one of ambiguity and paradox," of confusion of "all customary categories," echoes Jung's explanation of an individual in denial of her shadow and projections (50).

Another parallel can be found in Turner's description of an individual who is denied aggregation (the final stage of rites of passage), which mirrors Jung's account of people who are unable to achieve individuation. When aggregation or the reintegration process does not take place, liminality becomes permanent, which can also become very dangerous. This is the darker side of liminality, which may produce "undifferentiated monsters" who have not had the necessary rituals conducted when they have experienced a major stage in life (49). They become the unsavoury agonistic side of the community, the dark mirror of humanity. This dissolution of differences encourages the proliferation of the double bind.

Turner also suggests that a liminal state may become fixed,

referring to a situation in which the suspended character of social life takes on a more permanent character. The idea of a fixed state in a rite of passage has been defined as "permanent liminality" by sociologist Arpad Szakolczai (40). In this concept of permanent liminality we see mirrored my concept of narrative captivity. But in defining the eternal madwoman as a liminal persona, we are also provided with ways in which we can release her from permanent liminality and in turn narrative captivity.

Rupture line as borderline

As explained previously this book aligns itself with current academic discourse in critical disability studies, primarily that of Donaldson and Cahn and their approach to reading madness in literature. Not only is the eternal madwoman a narrative captive and a liminal persona, she is also a captive of a modern-day form of hysteria: borderline personality disorder (BPD). The model of the eternal madwoman and the ruptured narrative thus builds specifically on Cahn's exploration of border disorders and her argument that feminism and poststructuralism endeavour to break apart the unified self. The journey model and the arguments presented in this and following chapters, also build on Cahn's supposition that, while early feminist work on madness viewed mad women as "staging a valiant protest against the impossible constraints of a patriarchal society" (260), prioritizing the woman over the metaphor moves us away from the romance of resistance.

Furthermore, the writing technique that ruptures the journey model, the technique supported by the above feminist critics, creates a borderline: a threshold upon which the eternal madwoman sits. In this protagonist, we see mirrored the borderline personality disorder as female malady—what Cahn calls the modern-day hysteria—and the personality traits associated with this apparent disorder—the postfeminist (masculine) woman's anger and sexual assertiveness added to the hysteric's (feminine) emotionalism, irrationality, and craving for attention—which create a new recipe for madness. Just as Cahn argues that the Victorian hysteric emerges as the postmodern borderline, so the twentieth-century feminist novels explored in this book have reacted to the Victorian hysteric and her narrative experience with a new approach to writing her story that has created the postmodern borderline or eternal madwoman. Therefore, this new recipe for madness—this new narrative exploration of female madness—rather than rebelling against societal assumptions of, and constraints on women, actually reinforces cultural assumptions of gendered mental health and the social construction of illness. The eternal madwoman as borderline, in turn, plays into the hands of gendered images of mental illness, and the epithet as a sophisticated insult aimed primarily at women.

Just as, in medical terms, the diagnosis of BPD creates a pathologically disordered "character" as Cahn calls her, and affirms the power of today's biologically orientated psychiatry, so do feminist literary critics who interpret the eternal madwoman as a successful revolutionary figure add voice to this gendered character. The eternal madwoman (Esther, Antoinette, Narrator, and Nora) as borderline plays into the gendered criteria for BPD—"unstable self image, chaotic interpersonal relationships, emotional lability and marked impulsivity"—which create an "empty self" plagued by feelings of despair and loneliness (263). Just as the hysteric of the nineteenth century, such as the protagonist in "The Yellow Wallpaper," was viewed as a metaphor for rebellion, so, too, has the literary borderline protagonist been viewed as a metaphor for subversion.

Yet the eternal madwoman is female first and metaphor second. In this humanistic approach to the narrative, we see mirrored the experience described by Cahn in the memoirs of women diagnosed with BPD:

Constantly under siege, internally and externally, the authors describe a state of utter exhaustion, mental, physical, and emotional. But the struggle never ceased. Merri Lisa Johnson described the habitual nature of her torment, stating simply, "I choose hell again and again." (267)

The eternal nature of this hell, this descent into darkness, represented in the nadir of the madwoman's journey, demonstrates little personal or political efficacy. The space this eternal madwoman occupies can be seen to be the same as the conceptual space, identified by Cahn, that women use to try to comprehend their own bewildering psychic agony and solve their emotional conundrums. Thus, the issue remains that the authors of *The Bell Jar, Wide Sargasso Sea, Surfacing,* and *The Woman Upstairs* leave their protagonists in this conceptual space without a guide for the ascent out of their psychic agony. This is not a criticism of the authors (who would, with the possible exception of Messud, probably refute the claim that their characters are feminist rebels) but of the feminist literary criticism that celebrates the characters as feminist agents.

Just as the lived experience Cahn describes calls into question the uncritical use of metaphorical borders and boundaries by feminist scholars, so too does the female experience of the eternal madwoman call into question the ruptured narrative as successful feminist device. This analysis supports Cahn's arguments that the feminist literary critics who "figure borderlines and boundaries as frontiers of opportunity where, released from confining spaces and identities, women are free to explore relationships unencumbered by constricting categories and conventions" provide a misleading and romanticized view (276). Finally, I argue the questions with which Cahn leaves the reader are similar to those pose by Caminero-Santangelo—and are similarly (as-yet) unanswered: "How do we understand the interplay between the corporeal body and social environment in producing mental suffering? How do we collectively work to prevent, ameliorate, or heal severe emotional pain, especially when it is disabling and persistent over time? And how do we turn harmful gender bias into salutary gender insights?" (275)

As such, this book answer Cahn's call to reclaim "borderline" from its status as person or thing and use it instead as a conscious metaphor of space. In turn, I maintain my definition of the protagonist as an "eternal madwoman" rather than an individual who could be diagnosed with BPD. This borderline is represented by the rupture dividing the narrative of descent from the narrative of ascent, and that this creation of a borderline space also creates an eternal madwoman who is a captive of her narrative structure.

Narrative captivity: why the madwoman remains unresolved

By utilizing Jung's theories of the shadow and projection, and Turner's cultural construct of liminality, we can theorize that the eternal madwoman's narrative captivity is caused by the character's inability to acknowledge her shadow, withdraw her projections, or experience the necessary societal rituals for her rite of passage. Thus, the analyses included in this chapter and previous chapters allow us to elaborate three possible reasons why the eternal madwoman's journey remains unresolved:

1. *Omission of shadow.* Without the realization of the shadow, all real further psychological progress is blocked.
2. *Maintenance of projections.* She is unable to be conscious of her projections and, therefore, cannot take back consciously what she still casts out unconsciously onto the outside world. Consequently, she is unable to accept responsibility for her own inner turmoil.
3. *Absence of ritual.* The character does not experience the necessary societal rituals necessary to move her through the rite of passage.

In the entrapment of the madwoman at the narrative stage of descent, we see the woman as unable to move past the chaos, to transcend the turmoil. Indeed, she is unable to integrate masculine and feminine attributes so as to become a whole individual. Rather than being an act of rebellion, as many current feminist theorists suggest, madness in literature simply reiterates a doctrine of gendered behaviour–and ending a narrative with the female protagonist locked within this behaviour even more so. As Jung himself tells us, we have "dealt the devil ... [no] serious blow by calling him neurosis" (75).

Thus, the narrative structure used by writers of the twentieth and twenty-first century madwoman, what I call the eternal madwoman, encourages its protagonists to become trapped in a state of psychological and cultural stasis; as argued in the previous chapter, this state can be identified with that which Cahn calls "borderline." I also maintain that there is little opportunity for rebellion or resistance in this state of permanent borderline liminality.

Descent and ascent: necessary for narrative

As Campbell argues, the journey downward usually precedes a journey upward, an up-coming (*anados*) or a re-establishment of equilibrium. Campbell believes that these two narrative paths, downward and upward, are inextricably bound and that, together, they "constitute the totality of the revelation that is life" (*The Hero with a Thousand Faces*, 21). Similarly, Todorov argues that the two halves constitute the "very definition of narrative" and that without the second hemicycle there is no character transformation, and thus no narrative (39).

If we read madness as narrative descent (rather than dissent), then, it inherently alludes to the possibility of an ascent. As Jung argues, while "no one should deny the danger of the descent ... every descent is followed by an ascent ... enantiodromia" (375).

In turn, new narrative possibilities open up for the previously trapped character of the eternal madwoman. Consequently, by departing from the established madness-as-rebellion metaphor and questioning the narrative structures that support a character's resignation to extant power systems, there is potential for more constructive and hopeful resolutions to our feminist stories.

Ultimately, as explained in the introduction, I argue for a feminist literary criticism that focuses on improving the lives of everyday women and therefore aims to answer the questions:

- How do we move the eternal madwoman character out of her suspended state of hopelessness and construct the personal development necessary to progress the narrative past the protagonist's real or metaphorical confinement?
- How do we transform a female protagonist from an oppressed and marginalized victim of the patriarchal hegemony into a self-actualized, self-loving, self-respecting subject?

In later chapters, I answer these questions and call for a twenty-first century feminist literary analysis, and indeed literature, that writes critically and creatively beyond the madness and out of the attic. Only in this way can we resolve the literary madwoman's impasse and move feminist literature forwards.

How, then, do we construct a narrative that moves the character of the eternal madwoman past confinement and towards a more hopeful and self-empowering closure? And, consequently, how do we "resolve" the madwoman in a fictional text?

At this point it is important to explain the link between releasing the madwoman from the attic and Caminero-Santangelo's question of "resolving the madwoman." It is, in fact, writing the eternal madwoman's release from narrative captivity that provides the possible symbolic resolution of the madwoman in a fictional text, and that it is the reconstruction outlined in the following chapter that enables a writer to contribute to the transformation of gender ideologies.

Figure 4: The eternal madwoman's narrative captivity

6

The madwoman's ascent

To understand is always an ascending movement;
that is why comprehension ought always to be concrete.
(One is never got out of the cave, one comes out of it.)

—Simone Weil (36)

In this chapter I propose that by determining a literary practice (encompassing reading, writing, and critical analysis) that can release the eternal madwoman from the descent to the goddess stage of the heroine's journey, we will be able to respond to the questions raised by Caminero-Santangelo: "How can transformation of the ideologies of gender (rather than just resistance to them) take place?" and "How can the symbolic resolution of the madwoman in fictional texts contribute to such transformation?" (2). This approach will enable us to bring together the approaches of both American and French feminist criticism, insofar as they can both be applied to one study.

Firstly, however, it is important to explain why we cannot use Murdock's model and its ascent as a guide to move the eternal madwoman onward from her narrative captivity. The heroine's journey does not explain, specifically, what must take place within a character to move her on from the depth of her descent to the beginning of her ascent. This may be because the framework is not a literary one, and therefore serves a different purpose; yet, even if a model is not literary it would be beneficial to include such information. I believe this to be a significant gap in a framework concerned with such resolution—absent information that is important not only for constructing a counternarrative to the madwoman in the attic, but for any literary practice that follows.

Even if the heroine's journey contained information for character development, however, new steps in the journey would still need to be defined since, for this particular case, a specific and unique ascent must be devised. Just as reading madness in literature as *descent* rather than *dissent* immediately points to the possibility of ascent, so the identification of the causes of the madwoman's narrative captivity alludes to catalysts for her release. If the omission of shadow, maintenance of projections, and absence of ritual preclude her from narrative ascent, then we can hypothesize that it is the antithesis of these attributes that will enable us to enable the eternal madwoman's narrative release.

The eternal madwoman's individuation and aggregation

The word "individuation" comes from the Latin word *individuus*, meaning "undivided," and is used by Jung to describe the process by which different aspects of the immature psyche become integrated into a well-functioning whole. Specifically, the process of individuation requires recognition and assimilation of the shadow and the withdrawal of its projections. Understanding the shadow, Jung argues, can "act like a life-saver" (257). It integrates the unconscious—reincorporating the shadow into the personality, producing a stronger, wider consciousness than before. Acknowledging the shadow is a launching-pad for further individuation; without it, further withdrawal of projections and recognition of the animus is impossible. Therefore, the process of individuation can be identified as part of the antidote to the causes of the madwoman's narrative captivity.

It is also important to address my earlier identification of the eternal madwomen as a liminal persona and the subsequent denial of the character's aggregation. During the phase of aggregation, Turner explains, the person re-enters society, and assumes "a new identity that needs to be acknowledged, understood and accepted by either a culture, a community, or an influential cultural figure" (49). For the eternal madwoman to be released, therefore, it is important that she experience the societal recognition necessary for the reincorporation phase. This type of reintegration is only possible after the liminal has been accepted as a marginal experience that leads to a new, transformative relationship with the social structures of the culture. Just as reading *The Bell Jar*, *Wide Sargasso Sea*, *Surfacing*, and *The Woman Upstairs* using the model of the heroine's journey uncovered attributes specific to the eternal madwoman's journey, so does the analysis reveal particular ways in which the character must undertake individuation and aggregation if she is to be released from narrative captivity.

The key: unlocking maternal agency, unlocking the attic

The madwoman referred to by Caminero-Santangelo in her call for resolution is an eternal madwoman created by the rebellion of particular feminist texts against the narrative closure dichotomy of domesticity or death. This resistance also causes a separation between the female protagonist in this fiction and any form of agency, love, or empowerment. There is a rupture between descent and ascent, the private and the public, the theoretical and the practical. It is important to note that it is feminist literary criticism's interpretation of the madwoman figure as rebellious that is problematic; they have thrown the baby out with the bathwater, so to speak. I argue in this chapter that there can be, in literary practice, a way to resolve the usual relationship between the patriarchal hegemony and the construct of domesticity. This chapter, therefore, aims to reinstate the importance of the metaphorical baby while staying true to feminist objectives.

Recent approaches to maternal agency (Marie Porter and Julie Kelso's collection *Mother-Texts: Narratives and Counter-Narratives*, Andrea O'Reilly's *Encyclopedia of Motherhood*, and Judith Kegan Gardiner's collection *Provoking Agents: Gender and Agency in Theory and Practice*) enable us to respond both to the need for the eternal madwoman to undergo the processes of individuation and aggregation, and to the counternarrative's aim of transforming gender ideologies.[1] As defined in O'Reilly's *Encyclopedia of Motherhood*, maternal agency is the notion that mothering can be a site of empowerment and a location for social change for women. It also draws on the idea that agency provides someone with the ability and power to influence and control her own life (O'Brien, 698).

However, I and these maternal scholars argue—and I stress this as pertinent to my wider argument—that the concept of the "maternal" does not need to be restricted to a biological mother, mothers, or, indeed, women. I focus, therefore, on extending the definition of "maternal" beyond "motherhood" and the constraints of biological determinism. I also, as explained later, wish to reunite feminism with the term "maternal," just as feminists in the past have aimed to embrace the term "hysteria"; it is crucial for the future of feminism for it to embrace the maternal.

Maternal agency includes two important components: the

maternal, and agency. I have chosen to use Gardiner's definition of maternal as "behaviour that is guided by an orientation to care for the self and others in a way that empowers" (152). In this sense, the term "maternal" relinquishes all associations with biological motherhood. In defining agency, Gardiner explains that in individualist models, when agency is attached to the self and is conceived of as an element of psychological being, it is said to be an "individual's capacity for self-determination realized through decision and action" (25). I define "self-determination" as the power or ability to make a decision for oneself without influence from outside. Since "relationality" is the key concept in feminist thinking about maternity (Jeremiah, 12), the definition of maternal agency for the purposes of this book transcends essentialist terms. That is, rather than pertaining to actual mothers, maternal agency is a figuration that may serve as a paradigm of relating to others. This concept of relationality has also, interestingly, recently been linked to the process of individuation (Venn, 129-161).

I combine the approaches of O'Reilly, Gardiner, and Marianne Hirsch to define maternal agency as, "An individual's capacity for self-determination realized through actions of any and all people that grant legitimacy to one's feelings, refuse the role of victim, and are guided by an orientation to care for self and others in a way that empowers." This kind of agency, O'Brien argues, can be a powerful form of development, during which there is a unification of the unconscious and conscious, resulting in a deeper responsibility to support, serve others, and foster peace, wholeness, and integrity in the world. It is this form of maternal agency that Judith Butler argues holds the "possibilities of gender transformation" (3) and, in turn, the transformation of ideologies we require to answer Caminero-Santangelo's questions. Ultimately, it is the denial of the maternal that manifests itself through repression and projection and that sustains the eternal madwoman's narrative captivity. Therefore, for the eternal madwoman, the process of enacting maternal agency can be defined as one of individuation and aggregation.[2]

For this reason, the previous framework of the eternal madwoman has been transformed so that the initial "repression of the feminine" is the more specific and relevant "repression of the maternal." Certainly, this repression is represented in the analysis of *The Bell Jar*, *Wide Sargasso Sea*, *Surfacing*, and *The Woman Upstairs* and is parallel to the necessary maternal agency. Yet, in a narrative sense, what would need to occur for Antoinette, Esther, Narrator, and Nora to enact maternal agency? Or, in other words—when Antoinette is standing, candle in hand; when Esther is standing at the entrance to the asylum meeting room; when Narrator is standing watching Joe and the search crew; and when Nora is standing, consumed by her anger—what could happen in that precise moment to move the character forward towards the possibility of narrative ascent?

Though Murdock's model of the heroine's journey does not explain how a protagonist moves from descent to ascent, Campbell's original monomyth does refer to the "keys" to the hero's release as being the "termination of the old eon and initiation of the new" (*The Hero with a Thousand Faces*, 212). This change in perspective, he argues, must be the result of the cataclysm of a crisis. Therefore, for the protagonist to be shifted from embodying emotional stasis to enacting maternal agency, a sudden upheaval must occur that creates the desire for self-determination. Since I have defined self-determination as the power or ability to make a decision for oneself without influence from outside, I term the required upheaval the "Demeter decision."

In the tradition of the myth of Demeter, where a mother negotiates the (partial) freedom of her daughter by threatening a barren land, the Demeter decision is a choice the eternal madwoman must make that precipitates maternal agency. With this decision I aim to create not only a catalyst for self-determination but also a decision that literary theorists and creative writers (not just of novels but screenplays and other narrative forms) might consider in and for their own work.

I suggest, therefore, that to release the eternal madwoman from narrative captivity, the protagonist must be presented with a Demeter decision, one that motivates her to grant legitimacy to her feelings, refuse the role of victim, and care for herself and others in a way that empowers. Thus, Antoinette, rather than burning down the English manor that has held her captive, must realize she has the ability to walk out of the building and away from her captor. Esther must understand that the psychiatric institution is merely enabling her to bury the issues with which she must deal, and therefore must leave the asylum of her own volition. Narrator must decide to leave the island, and thereby start her journey to integrate her private and public spheres. Nora, rather than being consumed by rage at her treatment, must acknowledge that she is as much responsible for her situation as anyone else.

This embodiment of maternal agency would enable the eternal madwoman to realize in that threshold moment that there is hope for a more positive resolution, that only she has the power to effect that change, that she must effect it without playing the angry victim, and that she must effect it in the public sphere.

At this stage of the heroine's journey, Murdock has a beautiful phase in which she speaks of "taking a cap off your heart" (88). In this description, we see similarities with the need to grant legitimacy to one's feelings, since feelings that are not acknowledged do not go away; they go underground and bind us to the past. Interestingly, Murdock believes a woman at this stage "drags her bag of bones behind her," a close parallel to Bly's description of the "long bag." In this sense, it is important for the protagonist to acknowledge her emotions and true feelings. The ultimate goal of this stage is for the protagonist to feel as though she is enough as she is—that "everything I need is within me"—and, therefore, to be forced by the Demeter decision to embody Gardiner's self-determination. This threshold decision creates the desire for self-determination and unlocks maternal agency.

By enacting maternal agency, the eternal madwoman can unlock the doors of her narrative captivity and the confines of being an oppressed victim of patriarchal hegemony, and take the necessary ascending step towards becoming a self-realized, self-loving, self-respecting subject. As O'Reilly states, this ascendance does not necessarily mean success, but it does enable the maternal protagonist to begin the "struggle" towards empowered maternalism (805).

The second crescent: writing the ascent

Once the Demeter decision, which encourages the enactment of maternal agency, has released the eternal madwoman from narrative captivity, there are further steps necessary for her ascent. I propose that a combination of Murdock's model of the heroine's journey, Turner's notion of aggregation, and O'Reilly's components of maternal empowerment—agency, authority, autonomy, and authenticity—enables the construction of a feminist narrative and, in turn, a new literary practice for the twenty-first century. Importantly, while this framework can be utilized by creative writers in all mediums, feminist literary critics and literary critics in general can also use it to determine whether a novel can be held up as a truly subversive or oppositional force.

The following steps will be explored in detail throughout this chapter. I argue that this combination balances the elements of the descent identified earlier.

1. *Authority—finding the maternal mentor.* The protagonist must find a mentor to understand, accept, and acknowledge the protagonist's new identity and role within society.

This process allows the protagonist to learn from an experienced guide and develop her own authority.

2. *Autonomy—acknowledging the shadow.* The protagonist must come to be able to say of her shadow, as Prospero says of the monster Caliban at the end of Shakespeare's *The Tempest*, "this thing of darkness I acknowledge mine."

3. *Authenticity—recognizing and withdrawing projections.* The protagonist must take back consciously what she originally cast out and accept responsibility for her own inner turmoil.

4. *Empowered maternalism—integrating private and public spheres.* The protagonist must assimilate elements of her private and public life so that they are integrated and so that both halves are as important and respected as the other.

These stages work as a counternarrative to the maternal descent. The finding of a maternal mentor and subsequent authority balances the enjoyment of the external boons of success; autonomy, which allows the acknowledgement of the shadow, balances identification with the masculine; authenticity, which allows the withdrawal of projections, balances the projection of the animus; and empowered maternalism's integration of the public and private spheres balances the repression of the maternal.

Authority—finding the maternal mentor

Murdock (though not in her model) argues that the most important element for a protagonist to begin her ascent is a positive feminine individual—the heroine needs to be able to accept help, and to accept it from the right person. "The Heroine needs someone to help her make her ascent from the Underworld (like Ninshubur in the myth of Inanna—Inanna asked Ninshubur for her help in making her return). The fictional heroine needs a friend or mentor she can trust to help her cross the return threshold."[3]

Since it has been determined that maternal agency unlocks

the eternal madwoman's attic, I define a new type of narrative guide, the "maternal mentor." The maternal mentor is similar to Vogler's "mentor," who comes from *The Odyssey*. Mentor, in Greek mythology, was a close friend of Odysseus and, together with Eumaeus, was given the responsibility of looking after Odysseus's son, Telemachus. He was a trusted counsellor, in whose guise Athena became the protector and educator of Telemachus. In the anatomy of the human psyche, mentors represent the higher self—the wiser and nobler part of us. This figure also represents a protagonist's highest aspirations and is who the heroine would like to become if she persists through the ascent.

Although Vogler describes different types of mentors who serve various purposes at different parts of a narrative, the eternal madwoman's mentor is primarily a source of wisdom, gifts, and conscience, and aids the eternal madwoman in overcoming her fears. Since the mentor embodies the goal of the narrative ascent, the maternal mentor must exude empowered maternalism, as defined later in this chapter.

The maternal mentor, or "wise older man or woman," enables the protagonist to develop authority, defined here as "an influence exerted because of recognized knowledge or expertise." By sharing her experience and knowledge with the protagonist, the maternal mentor imparts the "gift" of authority. Gift-giving has often been part of the role of the mentor in mythology and is referred to as his or her "donor function" (Propp, 12). In Vladimir Propp's dissection of Russian fairy tales, he observes that donor characters give magical presents to characters, but usually only after the heroes have passed a test of some kind. The Demeter decision is able to act not only as a catalyst, but also as a sign that the protagonist is ready to receive the maternal mentor's guidance and knowledge.

This maternal mentor and a female protagonist is one of the

most significant feminist relationships missing from twentieth-century feminist texts, highlighted by *The Bell Jar*, *Surfacing*, *Wide Sargasso Sea*, and *The Woman Upstairs*. It would be an interesting subject for further research whether this mentorship role is, in fact, missing from the majority of texts written by women with a female protagonist. It is also interesting to ask the question, "Does the omission of such a relationship within these texts represent a missing relationship in contemporary society?"

Felski argues that "feminism is defined by a fundamental tension and interaction between individual and collective identity" (*Beyond Feminist Aesthetics*, 68). This approach entails an understanding of human beings, not as abstract and isolated entities, but as members of social and collective groups. The maternal mentor (or mentors), as a key component of the emancipation of the eternal madwoman, is significant, since the goal of the protagonist's journey—and the text—is an identity that is more or less explicitly defined in terms of a notion of broader female community, and it is this that can be said to identify the model as distinctively feminist. The figure of a female mentor or mentors, therefore, invariably plays a symbolically important role in the protagonist's development." This transference of

> allegiance from a heterosexual relationship to one of intimacy between women involves overcoming the negative value which women have been conditioned to place upon their own sex; the recognition of the other woman serves the symbolic function as an affirmation of self, of gendered identity. (Felski, Beyond Feminist Aesthetics, 68)

In this way, the maternal mentor plays an important role in the eternal madwoman's emancipation, since she represents a mode of being and being together.

Autonomy—acknowledging the shadow

The heroine's journey begins with the separation from the feminine; in the construction of the eternal madwoman's journey, we found that the eternal madwoman is rejected specifically by her mother. Murdock explains that if a woman's psyche "has taken up" her mother in a negative or destructive way (as the eternal madwoman character has) she splits from her maternal nature and has "much work to do to reclaim it" (9). One way of seeking to heal this wound is by renewing or transforming this initial relationship. Yet whether the daughter is able to do this or not, the most important part of this stage, Murdock argues, is the reclaiming of the negative mother within ourselves. As explained in Chapter 2, the "negative mother" that is part of the daughter-centric narrative is referred to here and throughout the book as a socially and psychologically damaging construct and not as a reality.

Interestingly, Murdock actually refers to this return as "reclaiming the madwoman" (148). To "take back the dark," the character must reclaim parts of herself—the mean, cruel, withholding, manipulative, jealous, and greedy attributes that she has learned to repress—and also to acknowledge that these traits, which she associates with her mother, are in fact part of herself. This stage is, in Jungian terms, her acknowledgement of the shadow. Taking back the dark for the character means "moving beyond shame to reclaim *all* of the feelings she hid from herself, no matter how frightening, so that she can find her authentic voice" (80). As previously explained, for the purposes of this book I use a definition developed from Jung and outlined by von Franz: "In the first stage of the approach to the unconscious, the shadow is simply a mythological name for all that is within me of which I cannot directly know" (Booth, 2).

In the journey's ascent, I link this acknowledgement of the shadow to O'Reilly's concept of autonomy, which I define as "personal freedom gained from self esteem." Influential women's rights activist Gloria Steinem has written extensively on the concept of self-esteem, and connects external revolution to an internal revolution of spirit and consciousness. In many ways, the journey I construct in this chapter is also a direct response to Steinem's argument for the transformational qualities of self-esteem and for "thinking about ourselves in circles, with the goal as completion ... progress through mutual support and connectedness" (16). I suggest that this is an essential part of the resolution of the eternal madwoman. While the protagonist has repressed the maternal at the outset of her journey, she also represses the feminine (or anima) as a consequence of these traits being deemed unacceptable by the other characters in her life. By acknowledging this shadow, the protagonist is able to achieve the autonomy that Gloria Steinem describes as "trusting our very selves, despite the educational and societal pressures that may denigrate" the maternal experience (16).

In a narrative sense, then, the meeting with the shadow is crucial to the development of the self and, therefore, of a character. The shadow is the guardian of the threshold who can lead the way to selfhood, symbolized by the mandala: the circle, the wheel with the vital centre. Here we can return to what Jung himself wrote:

> *The transition from morning to afternoon means a revaluation of earlier values. There comes the urgent need to appreciate the value of the opposite of our former ideals, to perceive the error of our former truth, and to feel how much antagonism and even hatred lay in what, until now, had passed for love.* (Jung, 74–5)

It is Jung's description of "revaluation of earlier values," the "urgent need to appreciate the opposite to our former selves" and to "perceive the error of our former truth," that is vital to this book and to the resolution of the eternal madwoman. For, in the construction of the ascent as a counternarrative to the eternal madwoman, there is required an acceptance of falsehood in external influences and, in turn, a development of autonomy.

Authenticity—recognizing and withdrawing projections

Once the protagonist has developed a new authority and autonomy—motivated by maternal agency—she is able to recognize and withdraw her projections. I link this acknowledgement to the development of what O'Reilly calls authenticity (805). As previously explained, the masculine and the feminine are not genders but archetypal forces. When the masculine archetype becomes unbalanced and "unrelated to life," it can become combative, critical, and destructive. This unrelated archetypal masculine can be cold and inhuman, and it does not take into account our human limitations. It demands perfection, control, domination; nothing is ever enough.

It is this masculine archetype that Jung calls the animus. Thus we see, in this stage of the journey, the madwoman's projections onto the cultural groups described in the previous chapter. The only way a woman can heal this imbalance is to bring the light of consciousness into the darkness. Here we see the need for the character to withdraw her projections and accept the "nameless, unloved parts" of herself. Part of this process is to quieten the *machismo*, the voice inside that says, "I can tough it out, I'm strong, I don't need any help, I'm self-sufficient." The madwoman must stop seeing the other as the enemy, she must stop rationalizing her criticism, judgement and the polarization she creates by arrogantly saying she is always correct. Murdock argues that, at this stage of a fictional text,

> *the heroine must take a good look at herself to heal the wounded masculine. A best male friend who is wounded in some way himself might be one approach (for example, a male friend who has trouble*

with intimacy, or a male friend who is very controlling). Another would be the death of her father so that the heroine can look at how much alike she was to him, or how he held her back creatively, or how her relationship with him prevented her from having an intimate relationship with a partner (male or female).[4]

Indeed, this *machismo* is also the patriarchal voice of societal expectations that prevents the protagonist from being true to herself. I have chosen to define authenticity as "the ability to make decisions that are consistent with her own beliefs and values." Yet, until this point, the protagonist has been unable to identify, understand, or respect her true feelings. Through the enactment of maternal agency, authority, and autonomy, the protagonist is now able to recognize and withdraw her projections, which leads to a better understanding of the self and, in turn, one's own beliefs and values. This new understanding leads to a new authenticity and, as Elizabeth Butterfield argues, the ability to "reject normative expectations of patriarchal culture" (701).

Empowered maternalism—integrating private and public spheres

Finally, the heroine must integrate her public and private spheres. She does this, Murdock explains, by having the "strength to set limits and the willingness to take responsibility" for herself and others in a new way (185). In this stage, I have defined these "feminine" and "masculine" archetypes as the "private" and "public" spheres, as I believe that it is by integrating these two constructs that the protagonist is able to complete the journey and achieve empowered maternalism.

"Maternal" is defined here as a figuration that may serve as a paradigm of relating to others; as behaviour that is guided by an orientation to care for the self and others in a way that empowers. Therefore, the term "maternalism" transcends reference to mothers and motherhood and refers instead to an attitude of "care, nurturance and morality" that can be applied to any individual, community, organization, or, indeed, to society. I therefore define "empowered maternalism" as the ability to employ care, nurturance, and morality to effect change in one's own life and in one's community.[5]

I have, very deliberately, chosen to use "empowered maternalism" rather than O'Reilly's "maternal empowerment"— firstly because, as O'Reilly argues, as an academic discipline "maternal scholars and activists have sought to define and develop a politic or theory of maternal empowerment" (63) and, secondly, because maternal empowerment has been defined specifically to allow "mothers to be the focal point of the theory and politic" (67). I believe it is important to maintain the use of maternal empowerment as a term referring to the oppositional stance that seeks to counter the many ways that patriarchal motherhood causes mothering to be limiting or oppressive to women. Therefore, I use the term "empowered maternalism" to transcend gender and references to motherhood and women.

By struggling to achieve empowered maternalism, and by bestowing maternal agency, authority, autonomy, and authenticity upon a female protagonist, a creative writer might contest, challenge, and counter not only patriarchal motherhood, but also patriarchal notions of how women occupy private and public spheres in general. This should be an important aim not only for feminist texts, but for narratives and stories containing female protagonists in the twenty-first century.

Furthermore, utilizing "empowered maternalism" in creative practice provides interesting narrative possibilities. For example, if the maternal journey transcends gender, how would an organization or board of directors make the journey outlined at the end of this chapter? How would a father? A male protagonist? I believe that this approach, by eschewing maternal empowerment, allows us to transform the gender ideologies discussed by Caminero-Santangelo. I also argue that the integration of the private and public spheres responds to the call for transformation of gender ideologies.

As previously argued, twentieth-century feminist literature often separated the public/private binary and in turn created what I have termed the eternal madwoman. As Claire Pomery argues:

> the deconstruction of the public/private binary has several implications. It has politicized women's voices in a way that has disrupted the unity of women. Second, the concerns of private life are now exposed to the public, allowing for public and political influence on the private life, specifically in the form of legislation. Third, the deconstruction of the public/private threatens the individuality of experiences of women as women. By looking at different models for gender equality within the private and public spaces we can begin to find a way these spaces can be reconstructed to achieve a gendered equality. (Pomery)

It is important to note, though, that—as Adrienne Rich argues —a blurring of the public/private boundary can lead to an increase in patriarchal control over roles such as motherhood (242). I suggest that an integration of an individual's private and public domains transcends this concern, and can enable the balance required for an individual's empowerment. This is why it is vital that the maternal journey does not depend upon male intervention to occasion the narrative.

Notes

1   It is important to acknowledge that texts such as *Textual Mothers/Maternal Texts: Motherhood in Contemporary Women's Literatures* (2010) provide a thorough analysis of maternal representations in literature. Rather than beginning with an analysis of the maternal in *The Bell Jar, Wide Sargasso Sea* and *Surfacing*, this book began with the concept of madness in feminist literature. This starting point then uncovered maternal research as a possible component of the madwoman's resolution. This is an important note as, I believe, this makes the maternal journey outlined in this chapter even more significant for feminist literary criticism and literary practice in general.

2   It is important to note here, due to the reference of the maternal later in this book, that in the theoretical discourse of the aforementioned French feminists Kristeva and Irigaray, the maternal occupies a central space. Yet, I utilise Marianne Hirsch's argument that these two women's maternal discourse remains "firmly embedded in structures of representation which place the mother outside or on the margin" (Hirsch, *The Mother/Daughter Plot: Narrative, Psychoanalysis, Feminism*, 173). For this reason an analysis of Kristeva's or Irigaray's maternal research is not included in this study.

3   This was Maureen Murdock's response to my question in an e-mail message from author, April 17, 2012. Interestingly it would be a great addition to her model.

4   Again, like the mentor figure, this response was gained from Maureen Murdock in an e-mail message and exchange from author, April 17, 2012. Again it is interesting to note that these points that she has raised in our email exchange would be valuable additions to her Heroine's Journey model.

5   This definition of empowerment is based upon Jodi Chamberlin's in "A Working Definition of Empowerment," *Psychiatric Rehabilitation Journal* 20, no. 4 (1997): 6.

6   Claire Pomery, "Redefining Public and Private in the Framework of Gendered Equality," *Serendip*, 2004, http://serendip.brynmawr.edu/sci_cult/courses/knowbody/f04/web3/cpomeroy.html.

7

The maternal journey

*Postmodernism has not theorized agency;
it has no strategies of real resistance
that would correspond to feminist ones.*

—Linda Hutcheon (266)

Ultimately, the intersection between recent maternal scholarship and feminist myth criticism identifies maternal agency as a possible key to the eternal madwoman's attic and enables us to reconstruct a transformational journey; as Heller argues, it is the maternal that "breaks down the barriers that divide genderized spheres" (21). Mapped as the eternal madwoman's ascent, this approach provides a counternarrative and not only completes a new framework for fictional feminist texts and creative writing narratives in general, but also provides literary critics and readers with a new lens for analysis. This reconstruction allows us to plot what I call the maternal journey. As well as providing a new way of reading texts that fail to resolve the character of the madwoman, this framework enables writers to transform protagonists from oppressed victims of patriarchal hegemony to self-realized, self-loving, self-respecting subjects. In this way, the maternal journey acts as a counternarrative to that of the eternal madwoman and responds to American feminist theorists' calls for new narratives on madness and the use of myth criticism in fiction.

The maternal journey model also directly responds to the call for research into the relationship between structure and politics and that therefore the concept of the maternal is paramount to a feminist literary practice. It is, in fact, the agency and empowered maternalism enacted within the maternal journey that can be understood as subversive. This suggestion is in direct opposition to the arguments of French feminist criticism that chaos and hysteria enact feminist rebellion.

As Hirsch argues, North American and European feminist writing has only been able to inscribe the female by further silencing one aspect of an individual's experience and identity—the maternal (241). I further Hirsch's argument by suggesting that it is the attempt by feminist writers to free their narratives from the dichotomy of domesticity or death through the use of madness that ultimately silences the protagonist's maternal identity; and that it has been feminist literary criticism's interpretation and celebration of this eternal madwoman that has been detrimental to the feminist aesthetic. Hirsch argues that the "maternal story" cannot be filled in because we have "no framework within which to write from her perspective" (240). Again, in another development of Hirsch's research—in which she asks that we try to imagine those maternal stories—I suggest a framework for authors to write and for feminist literary critics to read the maternal. It is important to note here that (as explained earlier) the maternal perspective and maternal stories are neither essentialist nor limited to biological, or even nonbiological mothers, but rather represent a mode of self care and care for others.

This framework is not designed as an essentialist prescription for reading, writing, and analysing about the maternal or, indeed, female experience in the twenty-first century. Rather, it is constructed and theorized to open a dialogue and a literary practice that provides more hopeful and effective narrative possibilities. With this maternal journey model, I aim to participate in a dialogue on reconceptualizing the dominant notions of madness and maternity within society, and to engage in feminist discourse by suggesting new ways not only to theorize and write maternity, but also to theorize, read, and write stories.

The maternal journey is a new, woman-centred narrative that challenges the madness-as-rebellion emplotment of women's lives. But does this maternal journey provide Caminero-Santangelo's symbolic resolution of the madwoman in fictional texts to contribute to the transformation of (rather than just resistance to) gender ideologies? I argue that, by pointing outward and forward, into social activity and political emancipation, but also backwards and inwards, into myth, spirituality, and the transformation of subjective consciousness, the model acts as a counternarrative that rejects madness as a symbolic resolution. In this way, the maternal journey resolves the madwoman through a monomyth structure that can be utilized both for literary practice and by more general readers and creative writers.

The model also enables discussion of issues such as those surveyed by Caminero-Santangelo, of how fiction about madness duplicates through its structure the essentialist thinking that identifies women with irrationality in the first place. Thus, the maternal journey does not just respond to a call for resolution, but supports a literature and criticism that improves the lives of real women, such as that for which Caminero-Santangelo calls:

> Instead of privileging the retreat into madness, then, let us privilege forms of agency, and of active transformation in all its forms, which women engage in. And, in doing so, let us open an imaginative space for women to be able to escape from madness by envisioning themselves as agents. (181)

Figure 5: The maternal journey

The maternal journey is the first feminist narrative model to resolve the madwoman; and, in fact, is one of the first approaches to madness in literature that preferences questions of narrative structure. In this way, the journey model adds to Lars Bernaerts, Luc Herman and Bart Vervaek's narrative threads of madness.[1]

Yet this particular thread is concerned with another reorientation of how we use madness in specifically feminist literature. The maternal journey thus demonstrates how a female protagonist can push desires and emotional needs into the public sphere, but still partake in linear, rationale narrative that breaks gender stereotypes. It is in this context that the maternal journey does not represent an essential female self but recognizes that women's positioning within existing social, familial, and ideological structures differs fundamentally from that of men. As Kathy Ferguson argues, "a theory of liberation must address the problem of achieving self knowledge that is not coloured by the definition of self which the dominant party prefers and is willing to enforce" (12).

French feminist literary criticism, by claiming the eternal madwoman as subversive, has enforced a gendered view of madness, one that fails to acknowledge that women's assignment to a distinctive feminine sphere has throughout history been a major cause of their marginalization and disempowerment. Certainly, this approach offers an ending other than that of marriage, but the madwoman's situation is just as much a form of imprisonment as the cage of patriarchal domesticity. The maternal journey, in contrast, opens the door to the cage; it demonstrates that in fact it is the *structure* that can demonstrate a path to self-knowledge that both reconstructs the relationship between the private and public spheres and builds a dialogue between American and French feminist literary criticism. In this way, the maternal journey enacts oppositional politics through the protagonist's journey of development, which evaluates assumptions of current ideologies against the specificity of women's experience. Furthermore, the female protagonist in this journey is a direct response to Felski's call for an "archetypal female subject, which provides an ultimate grounding for feminist knowledge" (*Beyond Feminist Aesthetics*, 73).

Therefore, the maternal journey is a fundamental formal expression of not only feminist literary criticism's and feminist literary writing's, but of women in general's awakening to selfhood, mobility, and influence in the world. What is proposed in this book is not simply literary innovation, doing something differently from the way it has been done before; not simply the breaking from patriarchal form, but something much more specific, much more targeted and not only much more feminist, but more humanistic in its function.

There is something inherently important in the arguments on both sides of the feminist fence. While it might seem that I am promoting an essentialist and didactic model of analysing and writing feminist literature, what I am actually doing is opening up feminist literary criticism to move from celebrating madness-as-rebellion to a pluralistic approach that includes and encourages narrative closures such as self-realization, emancipation, success in the public sphere, and even marriage and motherhood, as not only positive feminist acts but as more subversive than the current dogma. Since, as Felksi argues, we cannot simply assume that "any example of a marriage plot is bad news for women ... it is hard to make the case that every work of fiction that moves toward marriage is imposing a male-defined worldview on unsuspecting female readers" (107).

Certainly, Nancy Miller would disagree with me; in her view, arguments that women's literature must go beyond the scenarios of madness and that the "reclamation of suffering is the beginning its purpose is to discover the new world" threaten to "erase the ambiguities of the feminist project" (74). Yet, Miller's statement, made almost thirty years ago, was a reverse premonition, in that the opposite is now true: feminist literary criticism has focused so much on madness as narrative closure and on this technique as feminist rebellion that the ambiguities have not been erased but multiplied. We are now in a position where feminist literary criticism is so diluted that it seems to hold no power whatsoever. This is, in part, due to the belief that irrationality is subversion. Where I would agree with Miller is in the desire for negotiation that would create a "new social subject" (118); in fact, I argue that this social subject is the protagonist of the maternal journey.

What the journey model also provides is a heroic protagonist to respond to a current lack thereof. Feminist literary critics have rightly discovered an absence of a heroic female self-image. Women have been prevented from identifying themselves with the active subject of quest-romance because they have internalized an image of themselves as passive objects—and this is as true of the nineteenth-century female protagonist as it is for the romanticized eternal madwoman.

While I do not go as far as to define the maternal journey's protagonist as a "hero" rather than a "heroine," as Heller does, I understand her desire to define a woman as being "heroic" in the traditional sense; to be able to claim this for women. A women's quest must propose strategies for discovering authentic selfhood and for claiming the right to take her journey out into the world. Heller defines this as the feminization of quest-romance, but even more important is the emancipation of the eternal madwoman. In fact, the maternal journey is the direct answer to Heller's call for a form that speaks directly to a woman's changed position in the public sphere, so that the very concept of heroism can be critically scrutinized and redefined for a feminized age. As Heller argues, it is time to map the dark continent, the frontier of an individual female psyche, while understanding how her specific ties to community, family, and loved ones empower—

rather than restrict—her capacities.

Heller also argues that feminist literary criticism should concern itself with reclaiming the voices that have been relegated to absence. The eternal madwoman is just such a voice; even though critics persist in pinning her up as a feminist poster child, even though she is one of the most discussed characters in feminist—and, indeed, in general-literature, in fact those discussions reiterate female absence; absence from society, absence from political and personal efficacy, absence from self.

If there is a growing need for feminism to reflect upon the relationship between theory and practice, then the maternal journey can act as both a framework for feminist literary theory and a practice for creating a literary text. It is the union of these two acts that creates the greatest agency. Just as it is only by moving out into the world that the protagonist of the maternal journey is able to become critically aware of the limitations of the eternal madwoman's existence, so it is that by constructing the ascent and completing a new feminist journey model we are able to appreciate fully the limitations of the madness-as-rebellion motif.

The modern monomyth

The maternal journey in many ways represents a modern monomyth; a structure that has been missing not only from feminist literary criticism but from everyday women's lives. This framework demonstrates the current absence of female mentors, community and ceremonial ritual, and celebration of phases in women's lives and, in turn, argues that the reintroduction and reintegration of these elements into women's lives is vital not only for a fictional protagonist's emancipation but, indeed, for the readers' as well. Yet, as a mostly secular society, we have lost faith in the stories that guided us through troubled times in the past:

When the mask that you are wearing cracks, when you lose faith in it, you can have a regression in your psyche ... when a whole society loses its imagery, it can be in what called a wasteland situation. This is the situation we've floundered in for the past century or two. Nothing really means anything because the images our religions all refer to millennia past, and we're not activating the world in which we live. That's the job for the contemporary poet or artist. (Campbell, Pathways to Bliss, 99)

As explained previously, theorists promoting the use of myth believe that the function of story is to guide us through the universal transformations of life—collectively known as individuation—using archetypes, with their symbolic characters and patterns of behaviour. In many ways, this modern guide to living is missing from our society. Yet, if one looks at literature as storytelling, if one brings it back down to earth, then literature has a vital role it could and should be playing, but is not. The current deconstructionist approach to feminist literary criticism defines this approach as patriarchal and oppressive. The reluctance of feminist literary criticism to embrace myth as a feminist device has meant that female protagonists have been excluded from having a certain narrative power. Male heroes in the monomyth are afforded a more expansive sphere in which to develop. As Heller points out, "gender bestows upon men the privilege of representing whole communities, whole nations, or even mankind" (11).

I would also argue that this means women readers are also excluded from learning through fiction how to navigate into, and within, a more emancipatory and expansive sphere. If the enabling function of feminist literature should be to constitute alternative accounts of female identity that preference subjective self-transformation (Felski, *Beyond Feminist Aesthetics*, 152), then one must ask: has much of feminist literary criticism failed the woman reader? The maternal journey's protagonist shares the supreme ordeal—as Campbell declares, carries the cross of the redeemer—not in her brightest moments, but in the silences of her personal despair.

Even though there is much theoretical encouragement for myth-based fiction and feminist literary analysis, there is a lack of studies in this area. There is also an absence of practical frameworks for fiction seeking to have a positive impact on its reader. We are left to ask: where are the modern-day interpretations that translate myth's pedagogical function and provide guidance on "how to live a human life under any circumstances?" (Campbell, *Pathways to Bliss*, 31). Indeed, one can reword Campbell's quote to be specific to this study: where is the literary guidance on how to achieve self-actualization and emancipation as a woman in today's society? If the hero has a thousand faces and, as Carol Christ argues, "the heroine has scarcely a dozen" (9), then with this model I aim to contribute a few more identities to the feminist protagonist's face; specifically and especially, that of agent.

Yet, positioning the maternal journey as a monomyth does not mean that its protagonist is a universal woman subject, the sort of woman that can speak for others. Certainly no white, heterosexual, middle-class woman of European origin can speak for another woman who is none of these things. Yet, beneath such differences women do have something in common, something that they do not have in common with men of the same race, class, sexual orientation, or national origin (xiii). It is precisely the journey's relationship with myth, which bases its essence in primitive oral narrative. Like the folk tale that has been handed down almost to the present day, this narrative is modelled on fixed structures, on, one might say, prefabricated elements—elements, however, that allow an enormous number of combinations. Calvino puts it succinctly and poetically when he muses that even if the folk imagination is "not boundless like the ocean there is no reason to think of it as being like a water tank of small capacity" (6). The operations of narrative, like those of mathematics, he argues, "cannot differ all that much from one people to another, but what can be constructed on the basis of these elementary processes can present unlimited combinations, permutations, and transformations" (6).

Transforming gender ideologies

It is difficult to discuss gender in literature without mentioning Nancy Miller's collection of academics' essays on *The Poetics of Gender*. Feminist literary criticism has long been consumed by the debate about whether gender has a poetics. Though written thirty years ago, Miller's assertions that "the social construction of sexual difference plays a constitutive role in the production, reception and history of literature" and that "the very conventions and categories of critical discourse within which we all operate ... are inextricably involved with the conventions and categories of identity itself" (xi) remain pertinent today. I argue that the interpretation and celebration of the eternal madwoman as feminist rebel is gendered and reinscribes women in a position in the private sphere.

In contrast, the maternal journey provides a frame for drawing a diversity of cultural experience into the currency of signification, and is not simply an inverse of masculine norms but a questioning of the presupposed categories of gender. In this way, I add to the work of Heller on female quest structures and their ability to empower a female protagonist. By struggling to achieve empowered maternalism, and by bestowing maternal agency, authority, autonomy, and authenticity upon a female protagonist, a novel can contest, challenge, and counter patriarchal notions of how women occupy private and public spheres. This should be an important aim for feminist texts of the twenty-first century.

Thus, recent approaches to maternal research and, specifically, maternal agency enable us to respond to Caminero-Santangelo's argument for the transformation of gender ideologies by the symbolic resolution of the madwoman in a fictional text. Specifically, the maternal journey contributes to the trans-formation of gender ideologies by disassociating effective feminist rebellion from madness; by disproving the negative mother construct; by integrating the public and private sphere; and by defining and applying the maternal, maternal agency, and empowered maternalism in a way that transcends gender.

Of course, the interaction between gender and ideology in narrative form is vast, complex, and dynamic. The above list presents four possible ways in which a framework such as the maternal journey may reconstruct our beliefs about gender. It is, in fact, the reconstruction of the ascent and the descent, and the literary practice exemplifying this reconstruction, that has the potential to transform gendered principles. Rather than coding language as masculine or feminine and defining forms as gender-specific, the maternal journey, as feminist literary device for textual analysis and creation, questions the value of such categories and opens up the range and richness of existing and historical cultural traditions as potentially accessible and adaptable to the specific political and aesthetic interests of women.

In this way, I use terms such as gender, feminine, woman, and madness in the ways in which they are used in everyday language. Like Katey Castellano and other ecofeminists, I aspire to direct the message of feminist criticism back to a wider audience and to position theories of gender in a way in that respects and refers to the everyday experiences of gender rather than to institutionalized theories.

The maternal journey and ordinary language philosophy

The maternal journey model not only responds to Caminero-Santangelo's important feminist question, but is also the approach—argued for by theorists such as Moi and Felski—that provides

> *analysis of the subject which is not theoretically inadequate, yet which is able to account for the emancipatory potential of the women's movement as a politics that has been strongly grounded in the dynamics of everyday life, rather than seeking its primary legitimization in the subversive writings of an elite of literary theorists and avant-garde writers.* (Felski, Beyond Feminist Aesthetics, 54)

The maternal journey, grounded in the dynamics of everyday life, exemplifies an application of ordinary language philosophy. Whereas Moi applies ordinary language philosophy to "intersectionality theory," I apply the approach to my aim to resolve the madwoman in fictional texts and my argument for the maternal journey. As explained in the introduction, one of Moi's key focuses is on Wittgenstein's diagnosis of theory as having "a craving for generality." Theorists, she argues, in the grip of craving for generality, are interested in the general concept, not the particular case. I would argue that French feminist criticism and the uncritical celebration of irrationalism demonstrate contempt for the particular and render literary analysis of madness incapable of the kind of concrete, feminist frameworks that help make women's lives intelligible. In many ways, this is what disabilities studies argues for, theorists such as Donaldson and Cahn would benefit greatly from applying ordinary language philosophy to some areas of their study—such as the desire to realign literary madness with women's lived experiences of mental illness.

Moi argues that any effort to "reach the particular through the general will always fail"; that a "theory fuelled by the craving for generality will always reproduce that hallmark distance from actual human experience" (196). I argue that feminist literary criticism's endeavour to uncover emancipatory literature failed through its focus on generalizations, and that its celebration of terms that end up losing their meaning has separated feminist literary criticism and madness in literature from women's lived experiences.

Moi goes on to explain that ordinary language philosophy provides alternatives to essentialism; I would argue that it can also critique theories (such as madness as narrative closure being essentially subversive) while arguing that we can in fact free ourselves from the notion that concepts (such as narrative structures) are prisons that we must deconstruct.[2]

Specifically, Moi focuses on three features of the craving for generality that she argues are particularly relevant to feminist theory: (1) the tendency to require concepts to have clear boundaries; (2) the wish to emulate the natural sciences' understanding of what constitutes an explanation; and (3) the demand for completeness.

Firstly, Moi notes that current antiessentialism proposes no alternative view, leaving only two options: to assert or negate the essentialist view. In my resolution of the fictional madwoman and construction of the maternal journey, I partake in neither of these options. I do not position the maternal journey as essentially representative of the only path to resolve literary madness; nor do I position it as a model of all women's experiences. An anti-essentialist view would argue that the eternal madwoman and maternal journey model, based as it is on analyses of four novels, has no standing—no claim to theoretical significance—because I have not proven and cannot prove that *all* examples of novels with literary madwomen (or, indeed, any more than the four examined) can be described in exactly the same way. This is, of course, impossible; no concept will ever be able to account for all exceptions and outliers. Yet Wittgenstein provides us with an alternative, a different idea of how concepts work, that I employ across all of the analyses and models in this book: that not all instances that fall under a concept need have something in common. My reading of four texts using the heroine's journey framework is akin to Moi's that, when she provides a specific example of something, it is an invitation for other theorists to "look and see." The eternal madwoman's journey is an invitation to writers and theorists to look and see if this model can be applied to other texts—other novels from the twentieth century, novels from other centuries, novels with lesbian and transgendered protagonists, novels with protagonists of other races, cultures, communities.

The second feature is what Moi describes as a particular intellectual attitude that a new concept should subsume all past, present, and future cases. Certainly, the models within this book do not subsume all past interpretations of madness in literature; rather, they sit alongside them as another particular case that can be developed and reinterpreted by other feminist literary theorists, especially those who focus on class, race, or gender. Likewise, I do not argue that these models are the end of the conversation (alluding to Moi's next point) and that, therefore, there is no further analyses or work completed on resolving the madwoman in fiction needed. By employing ordinary language philosophy and resisting the seduction of scientism, I have been able to construct new models and new arguments where previously academics in feminist literary criticism have been shackled by their need to find an element common to all possible applications.

Finally, the craving for generality is, Moi argues, driven by a dream of completeness, which is another variation of the search for a common element. Wittgenstein wrote that concepts and expressions of a grammatical kind cannot be meaningfully subjected to the demand for completion. For example, I have proposed approaches to the terms "literary madwoman," the "eternal madwoman" and "resolving" the madwoman, yet do not claim to be satisfied that this approach is not only the singular appropriate approach but is all that is to be said on the matter—it is neither exclusive nor exhaustive. If someone said, "surely this is does not explain all examples of literary madwomen," or "surely this is not the only way one could resolve the madwoman in fiction," I would answer, "certainly not."

In this way, I present my analyses of *Surfacing, Wide Sargasso Sea, The Bell Jar,* and *The Woman Upstairs* as my argument for the eternal madwoman and my subsequent construction of the maternal journey as Moi's "network of criss-crossing similarities, constantly established and extended in concrete use" (203). Another term I explore with the resolution of the madwoman, and which can be criticized as being essentialist, is feminist narratology.

The maternal journey as postclassical feminist narratology

Feminism's reclamation of the term "hysteria" had, and continues to have, far-reaching implications for feminist narratology. The structural scepticism arising from the embrace of irrationality caused has prevented feminist literary analyses from performing useful research into narratology. In 1986, Susan Lanser described the contingent relationship between feminism and narratology, which she named "feminist narratology":

> *My ... task [is] to ask whether feminist criticism, and particularly the study of narratives by women, might benefit from the methods ... of narratology and whether narratology, in turn, might be altered by the understanding of feminist criticism and the experience of women's texts.* (1)

Lanser made this statement three years after Shlomith Rimmon-Kenan ended her widely used guide to narratology and narrative theory *Narrative Fiction: Contemporary Poetics* with resistance to the idea that her study could be an obituary. Since then, one can see reason for Herman's definition of a *re-emergence* of narratology (3), of which I would argue Lanser's work is proof. Yet, although there has been a narratological renaissance of late in the general sense, feminist analyses that include narratology are almost nonexistent in feminist literary criticism on either side of the divide. Therefore, narratology has had little impact on feminist scholarship, and feminist insights into narrative have been similarly overlooked by narratology (674). Lanser is one of the foremost academics in feminist narratology, and I aim to embrace and build upon her approach in this book. Although there has been a slight increase in the association between feminism and narratology (by theorists such as Robyn Warhol, Mieke Bal, Ruth E. Page and Marion Gymnich) and even one collection of papers edited by Kathy Mezei, *Ambiguous Discourse: Feminist Narratology and British Women Writers*, studies into feminist narratology are still in their infancy. As a consequence, there exists a significant gap—and, therefore, a significant opportunity for feminist literary criticism to explore the potential of narratology, of structuralism, and of myth to empower an emancipatory feminist literature that seeks to give, structurally, prominence to the depiction of women's experience.

Mezei's collection goes some way to bridging the gap and stands as a rare beacon of light in an otherwise darkened landscape. By demonstrating theorists' focus on the combination of feminist theory with the study of the structures that underpin all narratives, the collection also demonstrates the inter-disciplinary and disparate nature of contributions to feminist narratology. Many of the contributors argue that, until recently, narratology has resisted the advances of feminism because theory has replicated past assumptions of male authority and point of view in narrative. Unfortunately, as I have argued throughout this book, this perception is deeply flawed. I do not argue for the scientific aspirations of a high structuralism with its forbidding terminology, but any form of hybrid narratology must transcend the belief that structure is somehow inherently patriarchal and make use of classical narratological theory. "Postclassical" does not refer to the absence of this theory but, rather, to the presence of context.

While Mezei includes a long and useful select bibliography on feminist narratology, many of the works listed are only loosely associated with feminist narratology, and many in fact reinforce feminism's romance with deconstructionist skepticism and the disruption or transgression of phallocentric symbolic order. Many of these papers and texts, and indeed many works that are considered feminist narratology, should really be classed as feminist literary criticism. So how do we define this field of research? Mezei argues that the essence of feminist narratology is the study of "the context of how stories are told, by whom, and for whom" (2). Yet this definition aligns itself more closely with literary analysis than narratology. While context is instrumental to feminist narratology, it is only half the story; to call itself feminist narratology, academic research must engage with the classical and postclassical theory of narratology itself. Possibly this is what Mezei means when she describes "how stories are told," but this is not specific enough. I define feminist narratology as an academic practice that integrates gender as an analytical category into narratological processes and relates textual structures to the contexts of production and reception.[3] Importantly, I argue for a postclassical narratology, one that transcends the *exclusive* focus on textual features. Yet, although the systematic features of narrative discourse are not focused upon exclusively, they are still necessary to the practice of feminist narratology. It will be important to the future of feminist narratology to separate itself from feminist literary criticism (which is not to argue that this field, in and of itself, is not profoundly important). As Lanser noted twenty years ago, instead of worrying about the poetical improprieties we should welcome other efforts, much as biologists might "welcome the opportunity for deep-water expeditions or accounts of them"; and the future that she forecast, the time for worrying about "sifting the theoretical from the praxeological, the textual from the contextual, the narratological from the interpretative" (259), is now. Although the vast exploration of what feminist narratology could, would, and should include has been important, currently its plurality serves only to dilute an area of research that has yet to contribute fully to literary criticism. It is only by embracing diversity within the framework of a clear definition that current and future academics will be able to understand how they can contribute to the field.

This clarity will also enable a more rigorous practice that can engage in discourse with other hybrid forms of narratology and, indeed, with postclassical narratology and classical narratology itself. In this way, by questioning the assumption that narrative structure is inherently masculine and intrinsically oppressive, we will be able to more adequately intersect narratology and feminism to create new approaches to feminist literary criticism. To enable this relationship between feminism and narratology, feminist narratology must aim to accomplish three overarching goals—similar to those of David Herman's *Narratologies*, yet with consideration of issues of gender:

> *(1) to test the possibilities and limits of classical, structuralist narratological models to capture how issues of gender inflect the production and processing of stories, that is to assess what sorts of narrative phenomena such models can and cannot illuminate;*

(2) to enrich, where necessary, the classical models with post-classical (not poststructuralist) and feminist models, thereby coming to terms with aspects of narrative discourse that eluded or even undermined previous narratological research; and

(3) to achieve goals 1 and 2 through interpretations of particular (literary and other) narratives, thus engaging with Wittgenstein's ordinary language philosophy, and demonstrating the relevance of postclassical narratology not just for the study of literary and narrative theory but also critical practice at large.[4]

By focusing on these aims, feminist narratology can build upon its past scholarly contributions, filter feminist literary criticism from the more specific feminist narratology, and, most importantly, engage more fully with the field of postclassical narratology in general. The maternal journey provides an example of the ways in which postclassical feminist narratology can engage with classical narratological theory, while also considering context and, indeed, gender.

Towards a maternal narratology

Just as Lanser suggested a mutually beneficial relationship between feminism and narratology, so I suggest a symbiotic interconnection between maternal theory and narratology. In fact, bringing maternal theory and perspectives into narratology might reorientate feminist narratology. Many maternal issues—feminist mothering, domestic violence, adoption, outlaw mothering, breastfeeding, child care, and concepts and constructs of the maternal that transcend gender—impinge on the discussion of how narratology functions by querying subject positions, cultural formation, the laws of genre, and the universality and stability of narrative forms.

Although there has been much written recently on "maternal texts" such as Podniek and O'Reilly's *Textual Mothers*, and Porter and Kelso's *Mother-Texts*, there is certainly space for the specific nuances of narratology to be applied to maternal scholarship and vice versa. Maternal narratology also allows us to rethink and reframe feminist narratives and narrative closure. Analysis and frameworks of maternal narratology argue for empowered maternalism as a counterclosure—as what should be an alternative to the domesticity-or-death dichotomy. Yet there is certainly room for more alternative endings and, indeed, further structural and narratological analysis of the maternal within literary texts.

Notes

1   Lars Bernarts, Luc Herman and Bart Vervaeck, "Narrative Threads of Madness," *Style* 43, no. 3, (2009): 283. In this paper, the authors assert that although existing studies in madness in literature have approached madness from different points of view, in general, questions of narrative structure have never been at the center of attention.

2   For the purposes of my intersection of this study and Moi's work it is important to note that when she refers to "individual experience" I take that to also mean the experience of one protagonist in one book.

3   This definition has been informed by the work of Marion Gymnich, "Gender and Narratology," *Literature Compass* 10/9 (2013): 705–715.

4   Based upon the goals listed in, David Herman, "Introduction: Narratologies," 3.

8

Towards an era of reconstruction

Against the accusations by the traditional left that feminism was individualistic and therefore bourgeois, feminism produced a form of politics and analysis which has perhaps more than any other modern movement asserted and demonstrated the necessity of personal change. This is crucial because, unlike traditional forms of resistance, it was insisted that subjective transformation was a major site of political change. Indeed it was implied that significant political change cannot be achieved without it.
—Julian Henriques (7)

A dangerous assumption permeates much of current feminist literary criticism: that narrative structures of any kind are repressive and represent a patriarchal desire for mastery and order, whereas the broken, ruptured, and borderline are feminine and, thus, supposedly feminist. It is not difficult to discern the hypocrisy in reaffirming gender stereotypes feminism should be refuting or the consequences of such relegation to the irrational for female protagonists. Yet this pattern, while leading to the celebration of the eternal mad-woman's journey, also allows us to deduce further disconnections. The deconstructive approach of feminist literary analyses has separated important relationships, created relational paralysis and prevented dialogue between important academic areas: feminism and narratology, feminism and psychoanalysis, and feminism and reader response theory. Over the past forty years, these dislocations have, unfortunately, severed feminist literary criticism from its historical meaning and relevance since, as Felski argues, "the defamiliarizing capacity of literary language and form does not in itself bear any necessary relationship to the political and social goals of feminism" (*Beyond Feminist Aesthetics*, 6). In turn, feminist literary criticism has been separated from what should be its primary goal: utilizing theory to better the lives of everyday women. As Annette Kolodny argued many years ago, although our focus should be on "the power of the word to both structure and mirror human experience, our overriding commitment is to a radical alteration—an improvement, we hope—in the nature of that experience" (17).

In many ways, deconstruction has been a necessary detour, enabling exploration of alternate forms and voices. However, as an approach it has also been damaging to the female subject in twentieth-century literature, and it is time to correct the imbalance. Furthermore, feminist literary criticism has had a tendency to focus on the past, and it is time to determine how we should journey into the future. With this in mind, I call for a new direction.

In response to the impact of deconstruction on feminist literary criticism, I argue for an era of reconstruction. Just as Showalter defined first-wave feminist literary analysis as a *rediscovery* of texts, and I have defined the second wave as a *reorientation* of the interpretation of texts, I argue for third-wave feminism's focus to be on *reconstruction*. As such, these three waves represent a picking up, a pulling apart, and a putting back together. Just as feminist criticism advanced by turning to the construction of a female literary tradition, and then deconstructing the historical scaffolding that supposedly prevented the identification of that tradition, so I aim to support the advancement of feminist literature by turning to the reconstruction of a female literary future. This immediate future lies in a focus on reconstruction rather than deconstruction. Since realistic conventions provide a steadier vehicle for feminist argument than experiments in nonlinear or impersonal techniques, an era of reconstruction that responds to the chaotic and open narrative techniques of the past will open up a kaleidoscope of new feminist narrative possibilities.

While in the past the textual practice of rupturing patriarchal forms involved what French feminist criticism believed to be the only radical forms—nonlinear, nonhierarchical, and decentring—it left unclear the nature of the relationship between the subversion of literary discourse and liberating transformation. An era of reconstruction defines narrative emancipation clearly and structurally in models such as the maternal journey and the reunion of feminism with academic areas previously—and wrongly—held to be essentially patriarchal.

Greene argues that this type of "symmetrically patterned, formally well-made" narrative's "neat, circular structure is finally constricting" (85). Although the protagonists find "an ending of their own," the sense is of a "narrowing off of possibilities rather than an opening up into new ones" (85). Yet it is in fact transcending paralysis, and developing empowered maternalism in the narrative, that opens up new possibilities. The maternal journey and, in turn, the reconstructed journey model, is therefore an important framework for not only feminist writers, but creative writers in general, in the twenty-first century. This era would organize discursive meaning around the projected liberation of an individual or collective female subject, generating a number of interpretations of the maternal journey, novels of emancipation set in the twenty-first century and the future, grounded in different conceptions of history and truth. An era of reconstruction thus argues for a differentiated understanding of structure as not constraining but enabling, a precondition for the possibility of meaningful choices.

In turn this new era could be a powerful subversive space and be used to call into question those more rigid intellectual schemata that, "by the very logic of their conception of language, serve to privilege the standpoint of the deconstructive theorist as the only genuine site of resistance" (Felski, *Beyond Feminist Aesthetics*, 54). This new focus for third-wave feminist literary criticism is vital for its survival, since we cannot continue to think in antihumanist terms. We cannot continue, surely, to argue that a female protagonist trapped in emotional distress is positive for feminism or, indeed, for humanity.

With an era of reconstruction, I argue for the power of narrative structure and the ways in which it can enable and empower emancipation. We are tired of being trapped, tired of being the victim. Happy endings need not be limited to mass-market fiction; they should be utilized by high-brow feminist literature as well. An era of reconstruction reunites the feminist protagonist with what she deserves: empowerment.

The celebration of the eternal madwoman's journey in feminist literary criticism as a subversive space that rebels against the patriarchal hegemony has prevented literary examples of positive personal change. This obstruction has also impeded the political efficacy of feminist literary criticism and the forward momentum of women's rights in literature. Yet, as previously explained, my approach is based upon considering both the French and American approaches to feminist literary criticism and, although overall aligning my arguments with that of the American side,

I believe that an era of reconstruction is as much about bringing both side of the feminist literary criticism into play as much as possible in analysis, rather than an either/or dichotomy.

I argue, therefore, for a new approach that embraces the importance of feminist writing as a medium of self-exploration and social criticism. In this way, an era of reconstruction does not simply aim to reconfigure relationships between feminist literary criticism and other areas of academia; it aims to repoliticize the literary text.

Storytelling is bound in *kathados* and *anodos* (the down-going and up-coming), which together create the total revelation of life. It is by journeying through these that one finds *katharsis*. Yet, catharsis with a "c" has other sources. Aristotle used the concept of catharsis in both the medical and psychological sense. In Aristotle's *Poetics*, it meant an emotional release and cleansing that has a corrective and healing effect. He believed that catharsis helped to moderate passions and strong emotions, therefore restoring the balance in one's heart. According to Aristotle, experiencing catharsis had moral and ethical implications. Catharsis has also been used in music, psychology, and counselling therapy; the main way in which it is employed in this book, though, is with Campbell's *katharsis* and the ways in which this rebalance reconstructs two halves. It is time that female protag-onists in literature—and, indeed, feminist literary criticism in general—experienced a catharsis.

This era embraces a narrative model of history as progress, emphasizing the activist and participatory dimension of politics and the necessity of engagement in the public sphere. The novel would then return to its function of charting the changing self-consciousness of women accompanying their gradual entry into the public domain.

Reuniting the private and public sphere

With the separation of the narrative descent from the ascent, we also see the separation of the private and public sphere. Twentieth-century feminist literature often separated the public/private binary and, in turn, created what I have termed the eternal madwoman. The deconstruction of the public/private binary has several implications. It has been argued that the theoretical and practical exclusion of women from the universalist public is no mere accident or aberration; rather, the emergence of a public sphere is itself intimately related to women's containment within the private domestic realm. This guarantees, as Felski argues, the "unity and cohesion of the rational discursive public and contains desires and emotional needs within the private sphere" (*Beyond Feminist Aesthetics*, 72). Deconstruction has also politicized women's voices in a way that has disrupted the unity of women and threatens the individuality of experiences of women as women. This structure—or, I would argue, lack thereof—leaves feminism no means of legitimating its own oppositional position. From this perspective, it is possible to indicate some of the difficulties that arise from a privileging of madness as rebellion as the foundation for a political aesthetic. In fact, this narrative structure traps women in the private sphere.

As discussed earlier, weakening the boundary between public and private spheres can have the opposite effect, resulting in even stronger patriarchal control over female roles, including motherhood. However, the protagonist's integration of their private and public—without male intervention—provides the path upward to empowerment. In an era of reconstruction, the self-actualized heroine would be given preference in feminist literary criticism over the eternal madwoman. In this new era, she must integrate her public and private spheres.

The maternal journey, which reconstructs the private and public sphere, is therefore similar to Felski's "feminist public sphere," which serves a dual function: *internally*, it generates a gender-specific identity grounded in a consciousness of community and solidarity among women; *externally*, it seeks to convince society as a whole of the validity of feminist claims, challenging existing structures of authority through political activity and theoretical critique (*Beyond Feminist Aesthetics*, 164). This sphere is also what Heller calls an "antifoundationalist coalition" that enables a "balance between selves and others, a balance where no community precludes another but ultimately understands itself and its own interworkings in relation to other communities" (122).

Reuniting feminist literary criticism with psychoanalysis

Just as deconstruction has severed the relationship between feminism and structuralism, between the narrative descent and the narrative ascent, so too has it cut feminist literary criticism off from dialogue with the supposedly patriarchal, oppressive perspective of psychoanalysis. In recoupling feminism with psychoanalysis, we can also reconnect the notion of literary madness with notions of mental illness, and with the disabling lived experience of real women.

I argue, along with Felski and Moi, that it is impossible to make a convincing case for the claim that there is anything inherently feminine or feminist in experimental writing and that, in fact, if one analyses the texts of *l'écriture féminine* the only gender-specific elements exist on the level of content, as in metaphors of the female body. Yet I take this one step further and argue that not only are there broad assumptions inherent in associating ruptured narrative with feminist rebellion, but that this structure of symbolic discourse both reinforces the very gendered representation of mental illness that feminism should seek to refute and entraps its protagonist in a position of powerlessness.

Reuniting feminist literary criticism with the reader

The impact of a novel on its reader has been one of the greatest omissions in feminist literary criticism. An era of reconstruction would also focus on reuniting novel with reader, critic with the real-world woman that the novel impacts. In many ways, this is a large part of the "feminist" component of "feminist literary criticism." If the past forty years have focused heavily on criticism, then an era of reconstruction aims to balance this perspective with a focus on "literature" (structuralism, psychoanalysis, narratology, myth) and then also "feminism"— that is, the improvement of the lives of everyday women. As well as considering the ways in which a fictional protagonist represents a real woman (as argued throughout this book), we also must consider the reader as the real woman who should be at the heart of feminist literary criticism. Just as Boyd argues that literary theory's focus on theory with a capital T has "isolated literary criticism from the rest of modern thought and alienated literary studies even from literature itself" and thus "severed literature from three dimensional life" (384–85), so feminist literary criticism's focus on critical theory has ruptured the relationship between literature and the real world, with far-reaching consequences.

Evidence has begun to arise that reading fiction activates the mind in ways that partly mimic direct action. Social neuroscience has also begun to discover how our minds can be affected by emotional contagion, by responding, even nonconsciously, to cues of specific actions or emotions in others—for example, a fictional protagonist. As Boyd notes,

> fiction is even more central to human life than we feel from the moment we first engage in pretend play to the moment we finish our last story. Although people continue to write and read literature with pleasure and passion, academic literary study over the past

few decades has often felt on the defensive, at least about literature,
as if it were a peripheral indulgence ... but if storytelling sharpens
our social cognition, prompts us to reconsider human experience ...
literary studies need not apologise. (384)

We can read between the lines of Boyd's quotation a similar relationship between feminist literary criticism and literature; and, indeed, a reluctance of French feminist criticism and the deconstructionist approach to view the act of storytelling, and its impact on a reader, as important.

Felski argues that, when anyone describes the essence of the human, it sounds almost naïve and that feminists are "right to point out that such views reveal unwillingness to confront differences. That these differences are not minor, trivial, or superficial; they go all the way down" (*Beyond Feminist Aesthetics*, 15). Equally, however, one can look at storytelling, at its historical structures and uses, and decide that there is something universal in our need to tell stories, and to tell stories that are structured not only to make sense but so that people can remember them and tell them to other people. Certainly, it is nothing new to deploy that famous Aristotelian formula, holding that we are, *inter alia*, not just social or rational or political animals but that we are also rightly distinguished as narrative or *storytelling* animals. Beneath this macro universalism there is an infinite array of differences in the context, content, objective, and interpretation of the stories that arise from this universal desire.

Reader response theory (rather than cognitive narratology or narrative empathy) should be the link between art (literature) and feminism; this connection is what will make feminist literary criticism more relevant and, indeed, increase the positive impact of literature in the twenty-first century. Reader response theory stems from hermeneutics; it is, as defined by Mary Klages, "the study of how readers respond to literary and cultural texts and emerged as a reaction against the New Critical insistence that all meaning was contained entirely in the text" (72). This approach argues that reading, making meaning, is an active rather than passive process; readers engage with texts and form interpretations based on subjective experiences. Some approaches to reader response theory examine responses from a psychological or psychoanalytic perspective; others look for "the social parameters within which interpretation takes place," arguing that "interpretative communities establish particular modes of reading" (72). Theorists who have developed this approach include Wolfgang Iser, Stanley Fish, E. D. Hirsch, and David Bleich.

One of the few detailed discussions of feminism and reader response theory is by Patricinio Schweickart in "Reading Ourselves: Towards a Feminist Theory of Reading." Schweikart argues that, referencing Showalter's identification of gynocriticism, "if it is possible to formulate a basic conceptual framework for disclosing the difference of women's writing, surely it is no less possible to do so for women's reading" (531). Schweickart contends that feminist critics should also inquire into the correlative process of reading: what does it mean for a woman to read without condemning herself to the position of other? What does it mean for a woman, reading as a woman, to read literature written by a woman writing as a woman? In fact, one of Schweikart's primary points is that it must be remembered that feminist criticism is a praxis, a political activity, its goal being not merely to interpret literature but to change the world in so doing. "Literature acts on the world," she argues, "by acting on its readers" (531).

This point, and the scientific studies of the effect of narrative on a reader's brain activity, certainly pose the question: what effect does the eternal madwoman have on a reader? If this trapped protagonist actually reinforces the precise gendered approach to irrationality and the isolation of women in the private sphere that feminism should be rallying against, then would a reader cognitively experience the madwoman's paralysis? Would she think it positive? And, to take this line of questioning a step further, does the lack (although presumably not complete absence) of feminist literature that travels a narrative monomyth such as that of the maternal journey signify that women readers are being prevented from experiencing forms of emancipation, however vicarious? As Boyd argues, "fiction aids our rapid understanding of real-life social situations, activating and maintaining this capacity at high intensity and low cost" and, in this way, "increases the range of our vicarious experience and behavioural options" (193).

The consequence of this new direction is a focus on the readers of feminist texts. The education of the protagonist is simultaneously that of the reader. As Heller argues,

> *when we read of women's quests, we become pioneers ourselves, drawn into unnamed regions by processes of imagination that challenge and expand our own psychic possibilities, our own potential as heroes.... It is humanity's quest to explore and understand collectively the myths we have only half seen and the powers we have only half-realized.* (123)

The need for powerful female identities is as important as ever. What we need is literature that does not just communicate current experience but that shows us what is possible. Once we have dismantled and reassembled the process of literary composition, the decisive moment of literary life will be that of reading. In this sense, "literature will continue to be a place of privilege within the human consciousness, a way of exercising the potentialities contained in the systems" (16).

By reading a novel that travels the maternal journey, a reader may themselves learn the journey towards self-realization. In this way, I adopt Gregory Currie's theory of "framework adoption" as a way in which a reader adopts a kind of attitudinal and emotional stance—in effect, donning a new persona at the invitation of the narrative itself and the way it is constructed.

It is a return to experiential rather than experimental texts, texts that focus on the journey of an individual woman, that actually rebel against patriarchal culture because they provide the greatest example (and potential for framework adoption) of female emancipation and, therefore, effective subversion. It is the reconstruction of the journey model in the maternal journey and the reclamation of the term maternal, that constitute a truly radical aesthetic.

The current popular strain of feminist literary criticism, which decentres the subject, can be seen as challenging the legacy of Western humanism. The maternal journey is a legitimating framework that can provide an objective foundation for human activities and would herald an era that aims to reconstruct the legacy of Western humanism as a space for feminist change.

Conclusion

Freedom and justice do wonders for one's mental health.
—Phyllis Chesler (44)

The argument that madness as closure is a counternarrative to happy endings, and is a more advanced structure because it disrupts ideological expectations, is persuasive but, on closer examination, reveals a number of problems that make it a tenuous basis for the development of a feminist oppositional politics.

I argue for a new optimism: a counternarrative that transforms a modern-day imagining of Bertha from an oppressed and marginalized victim of the patriarchal hegemony into a self-realized, self-loving, self-respecting subject. Simply put, I believe we should have the want and willingness to create a narrative structure that fights against the previous literary resignation. This kind of structure is what is missing in current and twentieth-century feminist writing in which the female protagonist remains trapped in madness. Thus, the ultimate objective of this book is to translate theoretical discourse into a practical framework for literary theorists and creative writers in all mediums who believe the incomplete, crescent-shaped life should not suffice.

I acknowledge the pluralist nature of feminism and do not aim at a single, reductionist model to be applied to the reading and writing of all feminist literature. The maternal journey is but one example of a model that preferences the self-realization of the female protagonist over the madness-as-rebellion metaphor. This approach, this reconstruction of the descent with a corresponding ascent, could be theorized in many ways and merely represents a change in how we approach feminist literary criticism and, therefore, the way in which we approach our politics. One effective indicator, perhaps, of whether a feminist theory and text succeeds is whether we would want our daughters to subscribe to it; and I know I would be reluctant for my daughters to believe in any form of "madness" as a state of personal and political emancipation worthy of celebration.

The current strand of feminist literary criticism advocates losing the plot; it celebrates irrationality and decries narrative structure as patriarchal oppression. I argue for a new era of reconstruction, of a return to literature as storytelling and an understanding of structure as human rather than masculine. I argue for finding the plot, and that, by embracing feminist narrative structure, we will have firm-enough ground on which to move forward.

This book enters a contentious academic world; not only feminist literary criticism but literary studies in general are being questioned in regard to their relevance. The two most vocal critics of the current state of literary analysis—and advocates of the scientific study of literature—are Jonathan Gottschall and Joseph Carroll. Both argue that there is a current malaise in academic literary study, what Jonathan Kramnick calls a "weariness that borders on hostility to the current state of the humanities" (317). Gottschall's most recent contribution to the field, *Literature, Science and a New Humanities*, argues that literary studies is guilty of an inability to contribute new knowledge, "real knowledge, knowledge that is consilient with the broader world of empirical research" (187).

Feminist literary criticism is uniquely placed to respond to the current malaise, but not by integrating literary studies with a scientific approach; in fact, I argue for precisely the opposite. By engaging with ordinary language philosophy, and by reuniting literature with storytelling (not simply the evolutionary approach), I believe feminist literary criticism can demonstrate how literary analyses can reconnect with the real world and, in turn, reassert its relevance. This approach is at direct odds with a scientific approach, which would focus on what Wittgenstein describes as a craving for generality. Feminist literary criticism and literary criticism in general are better placed defining themselves against this thinking and presenting particular cases, as I have in this book, that can tell us something about the wider literary landscape and the world around us—precisely as academics such as Gilbert and Gubar did before they were so heavily criticized and this approach was effectively silenced.

The humanities was named so for a reason. Yet, in the split of the narrative ascent and descent we see represented many of academe's divisions: theoretical/practical, textual/experiential, masculine/feminine writing. Yet we also see a larger and more telling societal split—that between academia and the real world, and then between the individual and the community. The argument that Campbell makes in his 1949 epilogue seems even more relevant in today's age:

> *today no meaning is in the group—none in the world: all is in the individual. But there the meaning is absolutely unconscious. One does not know toward what one moves. One does not know by what one is propelled. The lines of communication between the conscious and the unconscious zones of the human psyche have all been cut, and we have been split in two.* (The Hero with a Thousand Faces, 334)

I argue that it is the humanities' responsibility to honour its namesake and to reconstruct the link between theory and practice, between academics and nonacademics, between the general and the particular; and that this is best done by relinquishing the linguistically based and antihumanist notion that as the feminine is understood as a disruption of phallocentric symbolic order and, in turn, unshackling ourselves from what Moi describes as the "ubiquitous obsession with exclusionary concepts" (191).

Finally, I argue for a return to feminism and an honouring of the term's history and potential future. I argue for it in its singular form and for its presence to replace a silence where people are reluctant to use the term at all; yet, when used, it should be a word that encompasses a diversity of opinions and the nuances of particular cases. I argue for a return to the word "we," since "we" (any person who identifies themselves under the umbrella of feminism, and especially of literary feminist criticism) should be able to acknowledge our differences while retaining our definition. Maybe this is a focus for third-wave feminism? Just as Jennifer Baumgardner argues that the feminism she is inheriting does not represent her or her life, so would I say that the literary feminist criticism I am inheriting does not reflect my beliefs. In a letter to Katha Pollitt, Baumgardner explains that she had to realize that "older women didn't have an obligation to expand *their* feminism so that it defined me, but that I had the right and the responsibility to create a feminism that was relevant to my life and my values" (309).

Possibly the mandate of third-wave literary critics could be to recreate a community where there is presently division, and to reconstruct the division of dichotomies so that we are able to engage academically to provide concrete, feminist analyses that help make women's lives intelligible. Baumgardner would describe this new venture as being passed the torch; Pollitt would tell us to get our own damn torch. Either way, let us fuel a flame that lights the darkness, not only for our characters but for our readers; a fire that ignites literature that acknowledges the depths of despair, but that also identifies how this personal journey can be travelled—so that the next time a mother is in a bookshop searching for empowering feminist literature for her daughter, she may find everything she needs.

Bibliography

Adelaide, Debra. *Mother Love: Stories about Births, Babies & Beyond*. Random House, 1996.

Aristotle. *The Basic Works of Aristotle*, edited by Richard McKeon, Modern Library, 2001.

Armstrong, Nancy. *Desire and Domestic Fiction: A Political History of the Novel.* Oxford University Press, 1987.

Astbury, Jill. *Crazy for You: The Making of Women's Madness.* Oxford University Press, 1996.

Atwood, Margaret. *Surfacing.* Virago Press, 1979.

Auerbach, Nina. "Feminist Criticism Reviewed." *Gender and Literary Voice*, edited by Janet Todd, Holmes and Meier, 1980, pp. 258–68.

Balaa, Luma. "Why Insanity Is Not Subversive in Hanan Al-Shaykh's Short Story 'Season of Madness'." *Australian Feminist Studies* 29(82), 2014, pp. 480–99.

Baym, Nina. "The Madwoman and Her Languages." *Feminisms: An Anthology of Literary Theory and Criticism*, edited by Robyn R. Warhol and Diane Price Herndl, Rutgers, 1984, pp. 279–92.

Batty, Craig. *Movies that Move Us.* Palgrave MacMillan, 2011.

Baumgardner, Jennifer. *F'em: Goo Goo, Ga Ga, and Some Thoughts On Balls.* Seal Press, 2011.

Beer, Gillian. "Beyond Determinism: George Eliot and Virginia Woolf." *Arguing with the past: Essays in narrative from Woolf to Sidney.* Routledge, 1989, pp. 117–37.

Bernarts, Lars et al. "Narrative Threads of Madness." *Style* 43(3), 2009, pp. 283–90.

Berry, Ellen E. "Review: 'The Madwoman Can't Speak or Why Insanity is Not Subversive'." *Modern Fiction Studies* vol. 45, no. 4, 1999, pp. 1079–81.

Bly, Robert. *The Little Book of the Human Shadow.* Edited by William Booth, HarperCollins, 1988.

Bly, Robert and Marion Woodman. *The Maiden King: The Reunion of Masculine and Feminine.* Henry Holt and Company, 1999.

Bly, Robert. "Refusing to be Theocritus." *Neruda & Vallejo.* Beacon Press, Kindle edition, 1971, pp. 3–16.

Booker, Christopher. *The Seven Basic Plots: Why We Tell Stories.* Continuum, 2004.

Booth, Alison, ed. *Famous Last Words: Changes in Gender and Narrative Closure.* The University Press of Virginia, 1993.

Bordo, Susan. "Anorexia Nervosa: Psychopathology as the Crystallization of Culture." *Feminism & Foucault: Reflections on Resistance,* edited by Irene Diamond and Lee Quinby, Northeastern University Press, 1988, pp. 100–105.

Boyd, Brian. *On the Origin of Stories: Evolution, Cognition and Fiction.* Harvard University Press, 2009.

Brooks, Peter. *Reading for Plot: Design and Intention in Narrative.* Harvard University Press, 1984.

Brown, Daniel Russel. "A Look at Archetypal Criticism." *The Journal of Aesthetics and Art Criticism* vol. 28, no. 4, 1970, pp. 465–72.

Buell, Frederick. "Sylvia Plath's Traditionalism." *Boundary* 25(1), 1976, pp. 195–212.

Butler, Judith. *Undoing Gender.* Routledge, 2004.

Butterfield, Elizabeth. "Maternal Authenticity." *Encyclopedia of Motherhood,* edited by Andrea O'Reilly. Sage Publications, 2010, p. 701.

Buttrose, Ita, and Penny Adams. *Mother Guilt: Australian Women Reveal Their True Feelings About Motherhood.* Penguin, 2005.

Cahn, Susan K. "Border Disorders." *Disability Histories,* edited by Susan Burch and Michael Rembis, University of Illinois Press, 2014, pp. 258–82.

Cain, William E. *Making Feminist History: The Literary Scholarship of Sandra M. Gilbert and Susan Gubar.* Garland Publishing, 1993.

Calvino, Italo. *The Uses of Literature.* Harcourt Brace, 1986.

Campbell, Joseph. *The Hero with a Thousand Faces.* Third edition. New World Library, 2008.

Campbell, Joseph. *Meeting the Shadow: The Hidden Power of the Dark Side of Human Nature.* Edited by Connie Zweig and Jeremiah Abrams. Jeremy P. Tarcher, Inc., 1991.

Caminero-Santangelo, Marta. *The Madwoman Can't Speak: Or Why Insanity Is Not Subversive.* Cornell University Press, 1998.

Caminero-Santangelo, Marta. "The Madwoman Can't Speak: Postwar Culture, Feminist Criticism, and Welty's 'June Recital'." *Tulsa Studies in Women's Literature* vol. 15, no. 1, 1996, pp. 123–46.

Carrillo-Rush, Vanita. "Suffocating Under a Sealed Bell Jar: The Angel/Monster Dichotomy in the Literary Tradition." *Humanities Capstone Projects* 10, 2012, http://commons.pacificu.edu/cashu/1?

Castellano, Katey. "Feminism to Ecofeminism: The Legacy of Gilbert and Gubar's Readings of Mary Shelley's 'Frankenstein' and 'The Last Man'." *Gilbert and Gubar's The Madwoman in the Attic: After Thirty Years*, edited by Annette R. Frederico, University of Missouri Press, 2009, pp. 76–93.

Chamberlin, Jodi. "A Working Definition of Empowerment." *Psychiatric Rehabilitation Journal* vol. 20, no. 4, 1997, p. 6.

Chesler, Phyllis. *Women and Madness*. Revised edition, Palgrave Macmillan, 2005.

Christ, Carol. *Diving Deep and Surfacing: Women Writers on Spiritual Quest*. Beacon Press, 1995.

Cixous, Hélène, and Catherine Clement. *The Newly Born Woman*. Translated by Betsy Wing, University of Minnesota Press, 1986.

Cixous, Hélène et al. "The Laugh of the Medusa." *Signs* vol. 1, no. 4, 1976, pp. 875–93.

Cochrane, Kira Cochrane. *All the Rebel Women: The Rise of the Fourth Wave of Feminism*. Guardian Shorts, Kindle edition, 2013.

Cron, Lisa. *Wired for Story: The Writer's Guide to Using Brain Science to Hook Readers from the Very First Sentence*. Ten Speed Press, 2012.

Culler, Jonathan. *Structuralist Poetics*. Routledge, 1975.

Currie, Gregory Currie. "Framing Narratives." *Narrative and Understanding Persons*, edited by Daniel D. Hutto, Cambridge University Press, 2007, pp. 17–42.

Davis, Lennard J. "Seeing the Object As in Itself It Really Is: Beyond the Metaphor of Disability." *The Madwoman and the Blindman: Jane Eyre, Discourse, Disability*, edited by David Bolt, Julia Miele Rodas, and Elizabeth J. Donaldson, The Ohio State University Press, 2012.

Davison, Carol Margaret. "Ghosts in the Attic: Gilbert and Gubar's 'The Madwoman in the Attic' and the Female Gothic." *Gilbert and Gubar's The Madwoman in the Attic: After Thirty Years*, edited by Annette R. Frederico, University of Missouri Press, 2009, pp. 203–216.

Devereux, Cecily. "Hysteria, Feminism, and Gender Revisited: The Case of the Second Wave." *English Studies in Canada* vol. 40, no. 1, 2014, pp. 19–45.

Diamant, Anita. *The Red Tent*. Picador, 1997.

Donaldson, Elizabeth J. "The Corpus of the Madwoman: Toward a Feminist Disability Studies Theory of Embodiment and Mental Illness." *Feminist Formations* vol. 14, no. 3, 2002, pp. 99–119.

Doty, William G. *Mythography*. The University of Alabama Press, 2000.

Dow, Suzanne. "Madness in French Women's Twentieth Century Writing." *Contemporary French and Francophone Studies* 10(1), 2006, pp. 35–42.

DuPlessis, Rachel Blau. *Writing Beyond the Ending: Narrative Strategies of Twentieth-Century Women Writers*. Indiana University Press, 1985.

Edwards, Lee R. *Psyche as Hero: Female Heroism and Fictional Form*. Wesleyan University Press, 1984.

Eglinton, Yonge. *Feminist Literary Theory: An Introductory Handbook*. Textual Matters, Kindle edition, 2015.

Eisenstein, Zillah R. *The Color of Gender: Reimaging Democracy*. University of California Press, 1994.

Elbow, Peter. "The Uses of Binary Thinking." *Journal of Advanced Composition* vol. 13, no. 1, 1993, pp. 51–78.

Emery, Mary Lou. "The Politics of Form: Jean Rhys's Social Vision in 'Voyage in the Dark' and 'Wide Sargasso Sea'." *Twentieth Century Literature* vol. 28, no. 4, 1982, p. 425.

Estés, Clarissa Pinkola. *Women Who Run with the Wolves: Contacting the Power of the Wild Woman*. Random House, 1992.

Faludi, Susan. "Death of a Revolutionary." *The New Yorker* (2013), accessed 1 February 2016, http://www.newyorker.com/magazine/2013/04/15/death-of-a-revolutionary

Felman, Shoshana. "Women and Madness: The Critical Phallacy." *Feminisms: An Anthology of Literary Theory and Criticism*, edited by Robyn R. Warhol and Diane Price Herndl, Rutgers University Press, 1997, pp. 7–20.

Felman, Shoshana. "Women and Madness: The Critical Phallacy." *Diacritics* vol. 5, no. 4, 1975, pp. 2–10.

Felski, Rita. *Beyond Feminist Aesthetics: Feminist Literature and Social Change*. Hutchinson Radius, 1989.

Felski, Rita. *Literature After Feminism*. The University of Chicago Press, 2003.

Felski, Rita. *The Limits of Critique*. The University of Chicago Press, 2015.

Fowles, John. *Daniel Martin*. Little, Brown & Company, 1977.

Fraiman, Susan. "After Gilbert and Gubar: Madwomen Inspired by 'Madwoman'." *Gilbert and Gubar's The Madwoman in the Attic: After Thirty Years*, edited by Annette R. Frederico, University of Missouri Press, 2009, pp. 27–33.

Frankel, Estelle Valerie. *From Girl to Goddess: The Heroine's Journey Through Myth and Legend*. McFarland & Company, 2010

Fraser, Rebecca. *Charlotte Brontë*. Vintage, 1988.

Frederico, Annette R. "Introduction." *Gilbert and Gubar's The Madwoman in the Attic: After Thirty Years*, edited by Annette R. Frederico, University of Missouri Press, 2009, pp. 1–26.

Friedan, Betty. *The Second Stage*. Abacus, 1981.

Friedman, Ellen G. and Miriam Fuchs. "Introduction." *Breaking the Sequence: Women's Experimental Fiction*. Princeton University Press, 1989.

Frye, Northrop. *Anatomy of Criticism*. Princeton University Press, 1957.

Frye, Northrop. "The Archetypes of Literature." *The Kenyon Review* vol. 13, no. 1, 1951, pp. 92–110.

Gardiner, Judith Kegan, ed. *Provoking Agents: Gender and Agency in Theory and Practice*. University of Illinois Press, 1995.

Gilbert, Sandra M., and Susan Gubar. *The Madwoman in the Attic: The Woman Writer and the Nineteenth-Century Literary Imagination*. Second edition, Yale University Press, 1979.

Gilman, Charlotte Perkins. *The Yellow Wallpaper and Other Stories*. Dover Publications, 1997.

Gimbutas, Marija. *The Language of the Goddess: Unearthing the Hidden Symbols of Western Civilization*. Harper & Row, 1989.

Gottschall, Jonathan. *The Storytelling Animal: How Stories Make Us Human*. Houghton Mifflin Harcourt Publishing Company, 2012.

Gottschall, Jonathan. "What Are Literary Scholars For? What is Art For." *Style* vol. 42, nos. 2–3, 2008, pp. 186–91.

Greene, Gayle. *Changing the Story: Feminist Fiction and the Tradition*. Indiana University Press, 1991.

Greene, Gayle. "Feminist Fiction, Feminist Form." *Frontiers* vol. xi, 1990, pp. 82–88.

Gubar, Susan. "What Ails Feminist Criticism." *Critical Inquiry* vol. 24, 1998, pp. 878–902.

Gymnich, Marion. "Gender and Narratology." *Literature Compass* vol. 10, no. 9, 2013, pp. 705–15.

Harding, M. E. *The I and the not I*. Princeton University Press. 1965.

Heilbrun, Carolyn G. "Foreword." *Making Feminist History: The Literary Scholarship of Sandra M. Gilbert and Susan Guba*. edited by William E. Cain, Garland Publishing, 1994, p. xv.

Heller, Dana A. *The Feminization of the Quest-Romance: Radical Departures*. University of Texas Press, 1990.

Heller, Scott. "The Book That Created a Canon: 'Madwoman in the Attic' Turns 20." *The Chronicle of Higher Education,* 17 December 1999, accessed 2 May 2016, http://chronicle.com/article/The-Book-That-Created-a- Canon-/12650

Henriques, Julian et al. *Changing the Subject: Psychology, Social Regulation and Subjectivity.* Metheun, 1984.

Herman, David, ed. *Narratologies: New Perspectives on Narrative Analysis.* Ohio State University Press, 1999.

Herman, David. "Scripts, Sequences and Stories: Elements of a Postclassical Narratology." *PMLA* vol. 112, no. 5, 1997, pp. 1046–59.

Herndl, Diane Price. "The Writing Cure: Charlotte Perkins Gilman, Anna O., and 'Hysterical' Writing." *NWSA Journal* vol. 1, no. 1, 1988, pp. 52–74.

Hirsch, Marianne. *The Mother/Daughter Plot: Narrative, Psychoanalysis, Feminism.* Indiana University Press, 1989.

Hirsch, Marianne. "Unspeakable Plots." *Maternal Theory: Essential Reading,* edited by Andrea O'Reilly, Demeter Press, 2007, p. 241.

Hite, Molly. *The Other Side of the Story: Structures and Strategies of Contemporary Feminist Narratives.* Cornell University, 1989.

Hogan, Patrick Colm. "A Passion for Plot: Prolegomena to Affective Narratology." *Symploké* vol. 18, nos. 1–2, 2010, pp. 65–81.

Homans, Margaret. "Gilbert and Gubar's 'The Madwoman in the Attic' After Thirty Years." *Tulsa Studies in Women's Literature* vol. 29, no. 2, 2010, pp. 459–62.

Hudson, Kim. *The Virgin's Promise: Writing Stories of Feminine Creative, Spiritual and Sexual Awakening.* Michael Wiese Productions, 2009.

Hughes, Bill and Kevin Patterson. "The Social Model of Disability and the Disappearing Body: Towards a sociology of impairment." *Disability and Society* 12(3), 1997, pp. 325–40.

Hutto, Daniel D., ed. *Narrative and Understanding Persons.* Cambridge University Press, 2007.

Jacobi, Jolande. *Psychological Reflections: An Anthology of Jung's Writing 1905–1961.* Harper and Rowe, 1986.

Jenson, Deborah, ed. *Hélène Cixous: Coming to Writing and Other Essays.* Harvard University Press, 1991.

Jeremiah, Emily. "Motherhood to Mothering and Beyond: Maternity in Recent Feminist Thought." *Journal of the Association for Research on Mothering,* vol. 8.1–8.2, no. 15, 2006, pp. 221–33.

Joannou, Maroula. *Contemporary Women's Writing: From 'The Golden Notebook' to 'The Color Purple'.* Manchester University Press, 2000.

Johnson, Merri Lisa. *Girl in Need of a Tourniquet: Memoir of a Borderline Personality.* Seal Press, 2010.

Jung, C. G. *Letters.* Vol. 2. Princeton University Press, 1973.

Jung, C. G. "On the Psychology of the Unconscious." *Two Essays on Analytical Psychology: Collected Works of C.G Jung Vol. 7.* Translated by Gerhard Adler and R. F. C. Hull, Routledge, 1961, pp. 74–5.

Jung, C. G. *The Collected Works of C. G. Jung: Mysterium Coniunctionis, and Inquiry into the Separation and Synthesis of Psychic Opposites in Alchemy.* Princeton University Press, 1970.

Jung, C. G. and C. Kerényi. *Essays on a Science of Mythology: The Myth of the Divine Child and the Mysteries of Eleusis.* Princeton University Press, 1969.

Kaysen, Susanna. *Girl Interrupted.* Virago Press, 1993.

Keen, Suzanne. "A Theory of Narrative Empathy." *Narrative* vol. 14, no. 3, 2006, pp. 207–36.

Keller, Catherine. *From a Broken Web: Separation, Sexism, and Self.* Beason Press, 1986.

Klages, Mary. *Key Terms in Literary Theory.* Continuum International Publishing Group, 2012.

Klement, Kristine. "Feminism Beyond Hysteria: Reading Feminine Ethics." Psychoanalysis and La Femme, special issue of *Women Writers: A Zine,* 2010.

Knights, L.C. "How Many Children Had Lady Macbeth?" *Hamlet and Other Shakespearean Essays.* Cambridge University Press, 1979.

Kolodny, Annette. "Dancing through the minefield." *Feminist Studies* vol. 6, no. 1, 1980, pp. 629–75.

Kramnick, Jonathan. "Against Literary Darwinism." *Critical Inquiry* vol. 37, no. 1, 2011, pp. 315–47.

Kroll, Jeri and Graeme Harper, eds. *Research Methods in Creative Writing.* Palgrave Macmillan, 2010.

Lanser, Susan. "Towards a Feminist Narratology." *Feminisms: An Anthology of Literary Theory and Criticism,* edited by Robyn R. Warhol and Diane Price Herndl, Rutgers University Press, 1997, p. 674.

Leonard, Linda Schierse. *The Wounded Woman: Healing the Father-Daughter Relationship.* Shambhala Publications, 1982.

Lévi-Strauss, Claude. "Structuralism and Myth." *The Kenyon Review,* New Series, vol. 3, no. 2, 1981, pp. 64–88.

Lodge, David. *The Practice of Creative Writing.* Penguin, 1996.

Makward, Christiane. "To Be or Not to Be … a Feminist Speaker." *The Future of*

Difference, edited by Alice Jardine and Hester Eisenstein, G. K. Hall, 1980, pp. 96–100.

Mateas, Michael and Phoebe Sengers. "Narrative Intelligence." *American Association for Artificial Intelligence Report*, FS-99.01, 1999.

Mollow, Anna. "Mad Feminism," (2013), Social Text Online, 24 October 2013, accessed 26 February 2016, http://socialtextjournal.org/periscope_article/mad-feminism/

Meekosha, Helen and Russel Shuttleworth. "What is so Critical About Critical Disabilities Studies?" *Australian Journal of Human Rights* vol. 15, no. 1, 2009, pp. 47–75.

Metzger, Deena. "Writing about the Shadow." *Meeting the Shadow: The Hidden Power of the Dark Side of Human Nature,* edited by Connie Zweig and Jeremiah Abrams, Jeremy P. Tarcher, Inc., 1991, p. 301

Mezei, Kathy, ed. *Ambiguous Discourse: Feminist Narratology and British Women Writers.* University of North Carolina Press, 1996.

Micale, Mark S. *Approaching Hysteria: Disease and its Interpretations.* Princeton University Press, 1995.

Miller, Nancy K. *Subject to Change.* Columbia University Press, 1988.

Mitchell, Susan. *Icons, Saints & Divas.* HarperCollins, 1997.

Moi, Toril Moi. "Thinking Through Examples: What Ordinary Language Philosophy Can Do for Feminist Theory." *New Literary History* vol. 46, no. 2, 2015, pp. 191–216.

Mullan, John. *How Novels Work.* Oxford University Press, 2006.

Murdock, Maureen. *The Heroine's Journey.* Shambhala Publications, 1990.

Nicholson, Linda. "Feminism in Waves: Useful Metaphor or Not?' *New Politics* XII, no. 4, 2010, pp. 1–7.

O'Brien, D. Lynn. "Maternal Agency." *Encyclopedia of Motherhood,* edited by Andrea O'Reilly, Sage Publications, 2010, p. 698.

O'Connor, Erin. "Preface for a Post-Postcolonial Criticism." *Victorian Studies* vol. 45, no. 2, 2003, pp. 297–312.

Oliver, Kelly. *Reading Kristeva: Unraveling the Double-bind.* Indiana University Press, 1993.

O'Reilly, Andrea, ed. *Encyclopedia of Motherhood.* Sage Publications, 2010.

O'Reilly, Andrea, ed. *Maternal Theory: Essential Readings.* Demeter Press, 2007.

O'Reilly, Andrea, ed. "Feminist Mothering." *Maternal Theory: Essential Readings,* edited by Andrea O'Reilly, Demeter Press, 2007, p. 805.

O'Reilly, Andrea, ed. "Outlaw(ing) Motherhood." *What Do Mothers Need*, Demeter Press, 2012.

Payne, Michael. "Origins and Prospects of Myth Criticism." *The Journal of General Education* vol. 26, no. 1, 1974, pp. 37–44.

Pearson, Carol. *The Female Hero in American and British Literature*. Bowker, 1981.

Pearson, Carol S. *The Hero Within: Six Archetypes We Live By*. HarperCollins, 1986.

Plath, Sylvia. *The Bell Jar*. Faber and Faber, 1963.

Podnieks, Elizabeth, and Andrea O'Reilly, eds. *Textual Mothers/Maternal Texts: Motherhood in Contemporary Women's Literature*. Wilfrid Laurier University Press, 2010.

Pomery, Claire. "Redefining Public and Private in the Framework of Gendered Equality." Serendip, 2004, http://serendip.brynmawr.edu/sci_cult/courses/knowbody/f04/web3/cpomeroy.html.

Porter, Marie, and Julie Kelso, eds. *Mother-Texts: Narratives and Counter-Narratives*. Cambridge Scholars Publishing, 2010.

Propp, Vladimir. *The Morphology of the Folktale*. Second edition, translated Louis A. Wagner, University of Texas Press, 1968.

Rhys, Jean. "Letter to Selma Dias April 9th 1958." *Jean Rhys: Letters 1931–66*, edited by Francis Wyndham and Diana Melly, Penguin Books, 1984.

Rhys, Jean. *Wide Sargasso Sea*. Penguin, 1966.

Rich, Adrienne. *Of Woman Born: Motherhood as Experience and Institution*. Virago Press, 1976.

Rigney, Barbara Hill. *Madness and Sexual Politics in the Feminist Novel: Studies in Brontë, Woolf, Lessing, and Atwood*. University of Wisconsin Press, 1978.

Rimmon-Kenan, Shlomith. *Narrative Fiction: Contemporary Poetics*. 2nd Edition, Routledge, 2002.

Rody, Caroline. "Burning Down the House: The Revisionary Paradigm of Jean Rhys's 'Wide Sargasso Sea'." *Famous Last Words: Changes in Gender and Narrative Closure*, edited by Alison Booth, University Press of Virginia, 1993, p. 302.

Rodgers, Julie. "New French Feminism and Motherhood." *Encyclopedia of Motherhood*, edited by Andrea O'Reilly, 911Sage Publications, 2010, p. 911.

Rowe, Jessica. *Love Wisdom Motherhood: Conversations with Inspiring Women*. Allen & Unwin, 2011.

Roxburgh, Alan J. *The Missionary Congregation, Leadership, and Liminality*. Trinity Press International, 1997.

Russell, Denise. *Women, Madness and Medicine*. Polity Press, 1995.

Schweickart, Patrocinio P. "Reading Ourselves: Towards a Feminist Theory of

Reading." Gender and Reading: Essays on Readers, Texts, and Contexts, edited by Patrocinio Schweockart and Elizabeth A. Flynn, Johns Hopkins University Press, 1986, pp. 31–62.

Scholes, Robert. *Structuralism in Literature: An Introduction*. Yale University Press, 1974.

Schulte-Sasse, Jochen. "Forward." *Theory of Modernism Versus Theory of Avant-Garde*, University of Minnesota Press, 1984.

Segal, Robert A. *Why Are Mythic Heroes Male?* Lancaster University, 2004.

Shakespeare, Tom. *Disability Rights and Wrongs*. Routledge, 2006.

Shakespeare, Tom and Nicholas Watson. "The social model of disability: An outdated ideology?" *Exploring Theories and Expanding Methodologies: Where we are and where we need to go (Research in Social Science and Disability, Volume 2)* edited by Sharon N. Barnartt and Barbara M. Altman, Emerald Group Publishing Limited, 2001, pp. 9–28.

Shannonhouse, Rebecca, ed. *Out of her Mind: Women Writing on Madness*. Expanded edition, Random House, 2000.

Shen, Dan. "Why Contextual and Formal Narratologies Need Each Other." *Journal of Narrative Theory* vol. 35, no. 2, 2005, pp.: 141–71.

Showalter, Elaine. *The Female Malady: Women, Madness and the English Culture 1830–1980*. Virago Press, 1987.

Showalter, Elaine. "Gilbert and Gubar's Madwoman in the Attic After Thirty Years." *Victorian Studies* vol. 53, no. 4, 2011, p. 715.

Showalter, Elaine. *A Literature of Their Own: British Women Novelists from Brontë to Lessing*. Expanded edition, Princeton University Press, 1977.

Showalter, Elaine. "Twenty Years On: A Literature of Their Own Revisited." *Novel: A Forum on Fiction* vol. 31, no. 3, 1998, pp. 399–413.

St. Clair, Pamela. "In Search of the Self: Virginia Woolf's Shadow Across Sylvia Plath's Page." *Woolf in the Real World: Selected Papers From the Thirteenth International Conference On Virginia Woolf*, edited by Karen V. Kukil, Clemson University Digital Press, 2005, pp. 171–76.

Staal, Stephanie. *Reading Women: How the Great Books of Feminism Changed My Life*. Public Affairs, 2011.

Stange, Mary Zeiss. "Treading the Narrative Way between Myth and Madness: Maxine Hong Kingston and Contemporary Women's Autobiography." *Journal of Feminist Studies and Religion* vol. 3, no. 1, 1987, pp. 15–28.

Stanton, Donna C. "Language and Revolution: The Franco-American Disconnection." *The Future of Difference*, edited by Alice Jardine and Hester Eisenstein, G. K. Hall, 1980.

States, Bert O. "The Persistence of the Archetype." *Critical Inquiry* vol. 7, no. 2, 1980, pp. 333– 44.

Stein, Karen F. "Monsters and Madwomen: Changing Female Gothic." *The Female Gothic*, edited by Julian E. Fleenor, Eden, 1983, pp. 123–37.

Steinem, Gloria. *A Book of Self Esteem: Revolution from Within*. Little, Brown and Company, 1992.

Stevens, Anthony. *On Jung*. Routledge, 1990.

Storr, Anthony, ed. *The Essential Jung: Selected Writings*. Princeton University Press, 1983.

Summers, Anne. *Damned Whores and God's Police: The Colonisation of Women in Australia*. Penguin Australia, 1975.

Szakolczai, Arpad. *Reflexive Historical Sociology*. Routledge, 2000.

Todorov, Tzvetan. "The 2 Principles of Narrative." *Diacritics* vol. 1, no. 1, 1971, 37–44.

Tolan, Fiona. "Feminisms." *Literary Theory and Criticism: An Oxford Guide*, edited by Patricia Waugh, Oxford University Press, 2006, p. 328.

Truby, John. *The Anatomy of Story: 22 Steps to Becoming a Master Storyteller*. Faber and Faber, 2007.

Turner, Victor W. "Betwixt and Between: The Liminal Period." *The Forest of Symbols: Aspects of Ndembu Ritual*. Cornell University Press, 1967, pp. 46–55.

Van Gennep, Arnold. *The Rites of Passage*. Trans. Monica B. Vizedom and Gabrielle Caffee. University of Chicago Press, 1961.

Venn, Couze. "Individuation, Relationality, Affect: Rethinking the Human Relation to the Living." *Body Society* vol. 16, no. 1, 2010, pp. 129–61.

Vickery, John B., ed. *Myth and Literature: Contemporary Theory and Practice*. University of Nebraska Press, 1966.

Vogler, Christopher. *The Writer's Journey: Mythic Structure for Writers*. Third edition, Michael Wiese Productions, 2007.

Vries, Hent de. "Prefatory Note." *MLN* vol. 130, no. 5, 2015, pp. v–vi.

Walker, Steven F. *Jung and the Jungians on Myth: An Introduction*. Routledge, 2002.

Warhol, Robyn R., and Diane Price Herndl, eds. *Feminisms: An Anthology of Literary Theory and Criticism*. Revised edition, Rutgers, 1997.

Waugh, Butler. "Structural Analysis in Literature and Folklore." *Western Folklore* vol. 25, no. 3, 1966, pp. 153–64.

Waugh, Patricia, ed. Literary *Theory and Criticism: An Oxford Guide*. Oxford University Press, 2006.

Weil, Simon. *First and Last Notebooks*. Translated by Richard Rees. Wipf and Stock

Publishers, 1970.

Winterhalter, Teresa. "Narrative Technique and the Rage for Order in 'Wide Sargasso Sea'." *Narrative* vol. 2, no. 3, 1994, pp. 214–29.

Wittgenstein, Ludwig. *Tractatus Logico-Philosophicus.* Translated by D.F. Pears and B.F. McGuinness. Routledge & Kegan Paul, 1961.

Wolf, Naomi. *Fire with Fire: The New Female Power and How It Will Change the 21st Century.* Vintage, 1994.

Woolf, Virginia. "Men and Women." *Books and Portraits,* edited by Mary Lyon, Triad Grafton, 1979, p. 42.

Yalom, Marilyn. *Maternity, Mortality and the Literature of Madness.* Pennsylvania State University Press, 1985.

Zambreno, Kate. *Heroines.* Semiotext(e), 2012.

Zweig, Connie, and Jeremiah Abrams, eds. *Meeting the Shadow: The Hidden Power of the Dark Side of Human Nature.* Jeremy P. Tarcher, Inc., 1991.

Praise for *Finding the Plot*

A truly wonderful addition to both the scholarly and creative market. This book is not only groundbreaking in its theoretical propositions, but is also significant in its contribution to creative practice. The ideas behind the concept of the maternal journey are rigorous and well argued, and the resulting model for writers and story creators is a much needed addition to the creative canon. Dr Rogers will find herself sitting comfortably alongside the likes of Campbell, Vogler, and Murdock with this book!

Associate Professor Craig Batty, author of *Movies That Move Us: Screenwriting and the Power of the Protagonist's Journey.*

This extraordinary work seeks to heal the divisions between feminist literary critics in terms of how they understand madness, the interrupted heroic journey, "empowered (non-biological) maternalism" and transformation. Rogers brings an enormous erudition to bear on the compelling, controversial, and unresolved questions about fictional mad women in the attic, in the insane asylum, and in life, and what relationship they have and might have to both their critics and readers.

Rogers's goal—restoring the broken mythic and psychological connection between mothers and daughters in patriarchy, in fiction, and in feminist critiques—is creative and potentially healing. Always, what is missing in the novels she focuses upon, is a "maternal mentor," even or especially within oneself. Rogers understands that "privileging" madness as a feminist rebellion merely affirms the gendered "status quo." Daringly, she calls for "happy endings," which means both a descent into the "shadow" self and an ascent into self-esteem, and self-authored lives.

Brava Megan Rogers!

Phyllis Chesler, author of *New York Times* bestseller *Women and Madness.*

In this bold work of third-wave feminist literary criticism, Megan Rogers argues for a new way forward for fictional protagonists in feminist novels. She asks provocatively: "When did happy endings become so un-feminist?"

In addition, Megan Rogers has created a new concept — that of the "eternal madwoman" — and through her close reading of four of the best-loved mad-woman-in-the-attic novels (*The Bell Jar, Wide Sargasso Sea, Surfacing and The Woman Upstairs*) she encourages readers, novelists, and critics alike to envisage the possibility of cathartic "happy endings'" both in literature and in life.

Megan Rogers asks readers, novelists, and literary critics to re-evaluate a very old-fashioned term (one that has been devalued and is now ripe for renovation): the "message" of a novel. Her powerful call to arms is to assert that readers, novelists, and critics could find a use for theory "to better the lives of everyday women". Provocatively, Megan Rogers asks: Do we really want our daughters to be told that that being stuck in an attic in a state of madness and silence is an act of feminist rebelliousness?

As an alternative Megan Rogers envisages the possibility of a fictional (or a real) woman (one in pain) undertaking an emancipatory journey, out of "stuckness" and silence, towards a heroic ascent.

For Megan Rogers, finding the plot means a rejection of the valorisation of the madwoman in the attic as a rebellious victor. Finding the plot also means finding a resolution of the eternal madwoman's dilemma where she is stuck in a "descent phase" of aloneness, silence, and negation. Finding the plot means giving the madwoman in the attic the (self-)permission to come down the stairs, to no longer be silenced and to subsequently begin the "ascent phase" into being a "self-realised, self-loving, self-respecting subject".

Antoni Jach is the author of three novels —
The Weekly Card Game, The Layers of the City and *Napoleon's Double*
— and of the play *Waiting for Isabella*.

In *Finding the Plot: A Maternal Approach to Madness in Literature*, Megan Rogers challenges novelists to consciously eschew portrayals of the allegedly rebellious and feminist "madwoman in the attic" in favor of female characters who undertake a "heroine's ascent" to self-determination. She argues compellingly that it is not good enough for novelists to blithely place female characters who do not comply with society's gender constructs (mad women) into literal or figurative prisons (attics), and then equally blithely claim to have created a strong female protagonist. Instead, females in 21st-century literature who refuse the role of victim in a patriarchal hegemony must, she argues, undertake a journey towards self-realisation, self-respect, and self-love. But Rogers does not suggest that we make this an easy or comfortable journey, arguing that these female characters must, along the way, acknowledge their shadow, unify their unconscious and conscious selves, and accept responsibility for their own turmoil.

Thoroughly researched and convincingly argued, this is a study that should provoke all novelists to acutely review, and perhaps re-create, their own portrayals of female characters, and the narrative constructs in which they are placed. In rightly demanding that we discard easy pre-feminism female-victim archetypes from our narratives, Rogers has made a valuable and timely contribution to literary analysis.

> **Lyn Yeowart is a writer and editor, currently working on her first novel. As a result of reading *Finding the Plot*, she has rewritten the ending of her novel.**